THE PURPOSE CYCLE

THE PURPOSE CYCLE

UNLOCK THE SECRETS TO SUCCESS

BY JONATHON TUCKER

NEW DEGREE PRESS

COPYRIGHT © 2021 JONATHON TUCKER

THE PURPOSE CYCLE

Unlock the Secrets to Success

ISBN 978-1-63730-699-4 *Paperback*
    978-1-63730-790-8 *Kindle Ebook*
    979-8-88504-016-7 *Ebook*

To Sophie,

Keep up the
amazing work!

J. Tucker

Keep climbing

Table of contents

———

Sometimes, you're focusing so much on climbing the mountain, you forget to stop for a moment, look around, and realize how far you've come.

I spoke these words as my father and I were toward the summit of Scottish mountain Ben Nevis. It was a grueling opening to our UK Three Peaks challenge. When the going got tough, we stopped, observed our progress, and allowed ourselves a moment to reflect on how well we were doing. At some point in the process, though, you must push on further. My Dad spoke two words that I will always cling to for the rest of my life:

"Keep climbing."

I hope this book helps you toward success. Just know when you do get the sense of accomplishment, allow yourself the time to celebrate your wins, but remember to keep climbing—who knows how far this journey will take you.

This book is inspired by my hero, who still to this day tells me to keep climbing.

Also, this book wouldn't be possible without the adversity provided by those who gifted me many barriers to my goals.

I always say everyone has a book in them—and here's mine.

Introduction: What Is *Purpose?*

———

Vex King said in *Good Vibes, Good Life,* "Life is greater if you live with purpose. When you find a meaningful reason for doing what you do, you'll feel complete."

I always felt to be complete meant feeling a sense of fulfillment. What if this never happens? I was a young twenty-something British male wondering what my *Purpose* was. Asking yourself a difficult question is not the done thing. It certainly isn't "British" to philosophize about life or wonder what your *Purpose* is. The truth is, you're not supposed to have life figured out in your twenties—or so people say.

What if you have *absolutely no* direction? What if you lack vision? Brilliant! What great foundations to start from to gain a *Purpose.* You have a completely blank canvas. It's not like your parents are forcing you to take a career path or a relationship is stopping you from a dream job. If you are pigeonholed to one particular path in life, then you may remain oblivious to the glaringly obvious signals that life throws at you. Besides, very rarely do people who search for *Purpose* actually find it. It usually finds you. It could be an opportunity you can't refuse, a challenge that helps you discover yourself, or learning through loss—which is how I began to discover mine.

At the age of twenty-three, I lost one of my closest friends. Life stood completely still. Upon receiving the phone call to break the news, I knew I had to leave a difficult work situation and be around my friends. I had just started a new venture and signed half of my business away to a person I genuinely thought had the success I wanted to strive for... perhaps even a person I wanted to imitate in terms of success. However, in that moment of crisis, I quickly realized my *Aspirations* were all wrong. I was trying to be like a person who had his values aligned in the wrong place.

As I was making my way out of the office, he halted me and asked me a question I will always be grateful for: "What matters to you?"

I was trying to compare my priorities to that of a materialistic man. He had the watch, the car, the money, the relationship— everything I *thought* I wanted.

In that moment, I realized what really mattered to me: my friends and family.

He actually had everything I didn't want: arrogance, super-ficial values, and greed. What still matters to me to this day is not becoming that person. I had always had some form of discomfort during my life: a fear of being average. I knew I preferred the fear of being outside my comfort zone, which would eventually lead to greater things. Everybody should aspire to greater things. It's not a narcissistic trait to want to be extraordinary. In fact, we as a society often stifle people who push themselves out of their comfort zones. We ridicule start-ups, we criticize a person's weight loss, and we become jealous of a friend who bought a bigger house.

Once you start reframing these situations as signals you need to strive for *your* goals, rather than making excuses about "being dealt the unfair hand" or asking why that person you envy is so "lucky," then *Purpose* will find you. Things happen for us, not to us. So, use the energy as fuel to drive you down a positive avenue of pursuing your dream life!

Writer Annie Dillard famously said in *The Writing Life*, "How we spend our days is, of course, how we spend our lives." For many of us, a large portion of our days are spent at work. In fact, the average person will spend ninety thousand hours at work over a lifetime.

I have dedicated my career path toward serving my *Purpose*. That is, serving others as a teacher. If you are currently living for the weekend, does your current role you hate lead to greater opportunities? Are you prepared to persevere through a mundane working week if it results in you gaining the relevant skills and experience to ultimately achieve the job, the cause, and the "why" you have been working toward? I have certainly experienced both: working a job I enjoyed for not a lot of money and also finding a career path that started with difficulty, but I knew it would result in landing a role I love and progress to greater things.

Given the amount of time we spend at work, it becomes extremely difficult not to have your career related to your *Purpose*. Even if you feel like your career is completely separate from your vision, does your career not fund your goals? If that's the case, then it is related in some sense. You can then feel a greater satisfaction knowing there is a motive to turning up each day and contributing to your fulfillment. However, if this is not the case, then it may be time to reassess your direction and priorities.

Balancing the two is essential. Yes, your career and your *Purpose* should be very closely related—but this doesn't make money or materialistic possessions the goal. The Office of National Statistics states in a 2021 study those people living in London are reporting a lower rate of life satisfaction than ever before.

This just shows moving to a location doesn't make you successful. This is the misinterpretation of the phrase "Environment dictates results." Some people can become mega-successful by working from home, others require to move out of their hometown where they may have toxic memories. By environment, I mean your whole setup around you. This book aims to help you contextualize your environment and direct your life and resources toward your *Purpose*.

Purpose is relative, and it is not quantitative. Every self-help or personal development book I have ever read has taken me from "Point A" to "Point B." These books have helped me massively in developing myself in key areas of my life, but once I had arrived at "Point B," I was effectively finished with that book, and it gathered dust on the shelf.

The Purpose Cycle **is a repeating process that will guide you throughout your entire life. Growth is limitless, and so is your potential. As you improve yourself, you will begin a new cycle, and this book will be your reference to contextualize elements to your journey.**

Figure 1—*The Purpose Cycle: Aspiration, Realization, Initiation, Creation,* and *Fruition.*

The aim of *The Purpose Cycle* is to give you a framework in which you can relate to any of the steps along the way.

Whichever step is applicable to you at that moment will give you context and direction to help you. This book will be worth reading again and again as the stages can apply at various points, as well as the book being appropriate to cycles in different phases of your life. This could be a short-term *Purpose Cycle* or a longer-term *Purpose Cycle*.

The Purpose Cycle is a way we can consciously rationalize the seasons in our lives. The word "purpose" relates to direction and meaning in life. The word "cycle" implies life is not necessarily linear. Each chapter of this book can relate to a chapter in your story. You may have experienced these phases before, or perhaps you are yet to approach a particular stage. There are five stages to the *Purpose Cycle: Aspiration, Realization, Initiation, Creation,* and *Fruition.*

Purpose can be discovered through years of trial and error. In this book, I talk about many different microcycles, mesocycles, and macrocycles. These can be broken down into timescales:

Microcycles	Mesocycles	Macrocycles
1–6 months	6 months–36 months	3 Years +
Short-Term ambitions	Medium-Term ambitions	Long-Term ambitions
Small steps to success. Many similar microcycles can be tweaked and improved upon to form a mesocycle	Made up of Microcycles	Made up of many microcycles and mesocycles

Figure 2—The various timelines of life journeys we encounter. The seasons of development in our life equate to *Purpose Cycles.*

The idea is to go through as many microcycles and mesocycles as possible because then you will have built experiences to help you formulate what your true *Purpose* really is. It's almost like a "chicken and the egg" scenario. You need to go on many *Purpose Cycles* to understand your *Purpose*, and in turn, complete a macrocycle!

In addition to simply sharing this idea with close friends and family, my *Purpose* was born from a self-imposed "call to action" during the first UK lockdown in March 2020. The COVID-19 pandemic had detained the nation in their homes for months, and due to being clinically vulnerable, I had to shield. Being locked down affected people in many different ways. For my part, it was the best thing that had ever happened to me. As a schoolteacher by day, I continued to provide education online for my students while supporting my colleagues virtually, but I found myself with something I never had before: time. I also missed something I had always had: routine. Looking for something to get me away from the screens, I thought I would start committing myself to reading regularly. I would go to sleep filled with ideas after reading—so I began to write.

These two elements that called me to action—organizing my time efficiently and maintaining a routine during an uncertain time—enabled me to begin writing. But what for? What was the *Purpose*? I truly believe my *Purpose* stems from this book and delivering a message to as many people as possible. In my role as a teacher, I can affect the lives of a class of thirty children every single day. However, with this book, I could reach people across the entire world! I envisage this book leading to greater *Aspirations* further down the line.

Helping drive people's passions toward their dream lives is what I would consider to be my *Purpose*.

At the end of the school year, I always write a short speech to my students. The 2020s talk was about *Purpose*. It got me thinking, what happens when you find *Purpose*?

I have researched personal development for over ten years. Ironically, my first book was all about developing confidence when trying to build relationships with women (think the guy in *Hitch* and you're somewhere close!). Once I got the bug for personal development, I noticed the incredible changes I could find within myself—the addictive feeling of becoming a better version of me was constant encouragement to pursue it further. Having read a variety of books in various areas, the next step was to begin a podcast—*The Purpose Cycle Podcast*—where I have interviewed a range of incredible minds who have already taken themselves on a journey similar to the one we are about to embark on.

In these interviews, I have learned a great deal about what it takes to become successful, as well as achieving true self-*Fruition*. With my background as an educator, I have spent years helping children and young people achieve goals relative to the stage in their lives where they are at. This prompted my thinking. We all have goals that are relative to the stages of our life. Once you fulfill one *Purpose*, you find another and begin pursuing brand-new *Aspirations*.

The benefit of this is the more you know, the more you find out what you don't know. If you never push out of your comfort zone and experience many different cycles, then you will remain unaware of your potential. It could be blissfully unaware, or it could be unhappily unaware. Either way, I would rather be uncomfortable in a journey to find fulfillment than comfortable staying in one place. You have to pick your form of comfort. Mine is the understanding that through the unknown and bumpy roads, is the promise of growth.

The Dunning-Kruger effect discusses the paradox of framing life through the lens of a person who lives with a limited knowledge, low-challenge lifestyle, and is blissfully unaware of the situation they are in. Once they reach a point of knowledge, they realize the endless pit of wisdom that lies ahead. The stages of feeling overwhelmed, overcoming initial obstacles, and then feeling committed to learning more by developing intellectual curiosity is what entices you to delve deep into a subject (Dunning et al. 2003). I experienced these feelings when I first went into personal development.

THE DUNNING-KRUGER THOUGHT PROCESS

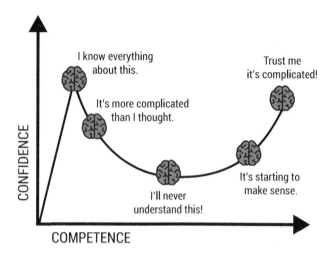

Figure 3—The Dunning-Kruger effect (Kruger et al. 2003)

We can *all* apply *The Purpose Cycle* to our lives in a host of ways. It is about rationalizing how we go through each stage and aiming to become better as we progress through life. In my time on this planet so far, I have lived many lives already. Situations would arise where I would think, "Why is this happening to me?" or, "How on earth has this occurred?" I couldn't contextualize the fact that things happen *for* us, not *to* us. Life dealt a good hand to everybody else but me—or so it seemed. Everybody has obstacles thrown at them—some more than others—but this is where *The Purpose Cycle* can enable you to understand a situation you are in, rationalize it, and act to progress forward in life toward completeness.

I relate feeling "complete" as a level in a video game. Any given area of my life has set parameters. I set the ceiling, or upper limits, but also the floor. To feel satisfied, I have to adhere to the standards and parameters I have set myself. These standards are part of my reason to wake up in the morning and *carpe diem*! My buildup of multiple short-term daily wins would ultimately lead to the contribution toward my macro-*Purpose Cycle*!

See, even your daily microcycles will ultimately affect you ten years later. Once I realize my potential from the momentum and the systems (routines) I have built, I set new standards for success and judge myself differently (almost as if I'm a completely new person) in this new situation than I did the last. This is moving up to the next level in life! The exciting element to this is similar to that of a video game player who is itching to get back on the game and fully immerse themselves in the process. Using this positive approach encourages me to view challenges and obstacles the same way I would playing a game. I embrace the adversity and enjoy the prospect of overcoming it to then reach my goal.

Truthfully, this book is for anybody looking to become an extraordinary, hero-in-a-video-game version of themselves. I'm not going to guarantee you a million-dollar income or to become the epitome of human physique. You'll have to do that yourself. This book is about giving you a framework to begin, achieve, then begin again, and achieve again.

I struggled with the ups and downs of growing up and the expectations of a changing world primarily dominated by social media culture depicting a perfect life—something I always thought I wanted. If you are in your early twenties and you, like the younger me, can't compartmentalize parts of your life, use this book to learn from my experience. If you are a budding professional striving to reach the top, use this book to develop a strategy that will take you there in your own time—not anybody else's. If you're just feeling lost and trying to find your place in this crazy world, then use this book to help find your way.

This book is for those people who are sleepwalking through their lives. If you wonder why things always seem to happen to you, then the biggest signal life has ever given you is to pick up a copy of this book. If you're reading this, then it's time to wake up. For those not reading this, the rest of us will leave you behind.

PART 1

ASPIRATION

CHAPTER 1

Lost

21

I didn't belong here. By this point, the bus was deep into the French countryside. The incredibly picturesque shades of green taunted a simple onlooker like myself. We were close to Spain, located somewhere in the region of Grands Causses Natural Regional Park, yet still so far from our destination. The annual university tour was much anticipated among the company I kept during this time. A lot had changed in how I viewed the world in the twelve months that preceded this installment of the tour. I had started my own journey in personal development after months of asking myself the same question: "What is the *Purpose* of my existence?"

The sights inside the bus were somewhat different from the artistic paintings surrounding the exterior: Beer being thrown around, shouting, singing (badly), and swearing. The internal voice of my "real self" that accompanied me throughout the trip begged me to just find a reason to escape. It was becoming increasingly obvious I was clearly the odd one out. The rest of the lads were as lairy as they had been since departing Teesside some thirteen hours earlier. My gaze out of the window was noticeable to Mark, one of my teammates.

"Oy! Tucker! What's up with you? You think you're too good for us, don't you?"

How do I answer this so they understand? I pondered.

In all honesty, I was past this phase of my life. There were very few occasions where I actually did feel a sense of belonging at university. It wasn't for me—the countless assignments, lethargically attending lectures, the "free-spirited" attitude of the people, copious alcohol, endless partying. I obliged the crowd because I assumed if I did this enough, it would become normal. Still, though I would fit in with the rest of the undergraduates who paraded campus, the thought of it terrified me. It was as if there was no turning back. On the other hand, I might eventually feel like a part of the tribe. One day, my initiations would suddenly be passed, and a sense of belonging would rush to me—either that, or eventually, the curtain would fall, the camera crew would leap into view, and I would be told, "This is all a hoax! Your real life is through that door!"

I perused my options of the rocky landscape surrounding us. We were approaching a small bridge, nothing like the grand towering presence of the Humber that always welcomed me home with open arms, a true sense of comfort and warmth engulfing me every single trip eastbound on the M62. This was so far away from home, but part of me wondered. Could this be a new home? A fresh start would be an opportunity to reinvent myself. I had a clear picture of what I wanted to develop in my life: mainly finances, health, and productivity. I was missing something, and I couldn't pinpoint what it was.

If the bus stopped right now, I could fake an excuse to go to my bags and just run. Location was irrelevant. It was my thoughts, my soul, and my being that needed belonging. Yes, I'm in France, and no, I can't speak French, but… I'll figure it out. There was a beautiful river below that meandered into the valleys. The sun was hitting the water at such an angle that it shimmered like a scene created by a movie set director.

"Oy! Think you're better, don't you?" Mark taunted.

"No… not at all."

"Who're you answering back?"

I didn't get Mark's problem. He was in my football team the year before, but now he had the attention of the entire busload of students, and he'd had a few drinks. There was clearly an agenda that had been built up, and he was ready to unload his troubles at that very moment. In my head, I was merely alumni, but my physical being was stuck on a stench-ridden, urine-soaked, beer flowing bus on its way through the heavenly scenery to what could only be described as four days of alpha-proving activities driven by booze, testosterone, and no care for anyone else on the planet apart from themselves. It was my own worst nightmare.

"Mark, leave it, mate, don't start anything," came a voice from the back of the bus. I was saved for now.

All the way through that journey, I felt two things: the first being Mark's eyes burning a hole in the back of my head the whole way to Salou, Spain, and the second, a real sense of not belonging on this bus. Mark clocked the fact I was uncomfortable. If I'm honest, the whole bus probably did.

Only a year ago, I was on this same bus headed to Croatia, but in a completely different headspace. I can look back and admit now I probably wasn't in a headspace at all. A drought of self-worth stalked my very presence, and the only sense of gratification my peers and I could gain was from telling each other how much "banter" we had. If I was a fly on the window of that bus looking at my past self, I would cringe—a young, naive Jon, admiring the chief jock of the football team, almost embarrassingly idolizing the guy. Everyone bowed down to him, even Mark.

During the year between that ride and this, a lot had changed. I had exhausted my stay in the university lifestyle and departed the region of Teesside for a host of reasons, one being the fact my three years of university had actually finished. I'd failed a module and had to retake that in the third year, resulting in my dissertation being the only thing that unshackled me from the education system for good (or so I thought at the time). My embarrassing lack of self-worth enabled the largest personalities to make their goals and ambitions my own. I had no clear concept of a vision and a complete lack of direction—seeking self-worth and guidance from perceived leaders was the next best thing.

Since then, however, I had shed the skin of zero self-worth, and Mark was incredibly aware of my newly found persona.

Watching Mark at this moment was almost parallel to watching a younger me, just begging for approval, so I pitied him instead of being upset. His *Aspiration* was misdirected. His motive wasn't for the values that would make him a better person. It was for the power that came with being the "alpha" of the bus. He was trying to impart his presence on the rest of us, and he saw me, his former football manager and elder peer, as a threat. By not laughing at his "banter" or pandering to his challenges, I was putting up a middle finger to him claiming leadership of the tribe.

Vex King in his book *Good Vibes, Good Life,* talks about the Law of Vibration. Essentially, the energy you put out into the universe is one that is obvious and typically (but not always) attracts an environment. Think along the lines of, "Your vibe attracts your tribe." From the moment I stepped on the bus this time around, it was evident my vibrations were aligned in a polar opposite manner to the previous semester. You could witness the displeasure and disgust in his eyes when he noticed my mindful absence on the coach. Minus the aggressive tactics, I could almost see a first-year freshman version of myself behind his exterior. Just somebody who wanted to fit in, belong, be respected, and be remembered.

University was not for me. It was lucky I was even there due to going through clearing (where your grades from A-Levels aren't quite good enough to get you into your first choices). If it wasn't for meeting a friend that ended up being "Best Man" at my wedding, I would've really struggled to find any joy from university at all. The football scene was heavily dominated by so-called "Alpha Males" like Mark, and my lack of maturity at the time led me there instead of passion. This is the first stage in which I can consciously remember my process through *The Purpose Cycle.*

What seemed like *Aspiration* in university was, in fact, admiration. I wanted to be like these guys—popular on campus, getting the beautiful women, and managing to keep on top of their studies. For some, this was the life they were chosen for—university celebrities. What I didn't realize at the time is that many of the roles you aspire to be in the hierarchy of the education's mini society are pointless in the long-term. The long-standing leader of the university football team, for example, ends up doing six years of university because he can't let go and becomes a nomad of the campus if you will. These roles ensure they never leave their bubble of security. They fear their wealth of authority, power, and fulfillment is based there and there only. How wrong they are! How wrong I was to think I could rebuild or reinvent myself at university to be like these figures. But it was needed; every step is needed.

It was incredible on my return to campus, following the nightmarish trip, to instead notice the people declared as "invisible" by those I had wrongly admired for a large part of my studies. These so-called "invisible" people worked their way through their studies, completing their course while building meaningful relationships with others and only seeking validation from themselves and their own achievements—not anybody else's. I have often beat myself up over having my priorities mixed up at university, but in recent years I have managed to be at peace with the regret of my former self. If I had not had those experiences and regrets of a younger, naive me, then I wouldn't be the person I am today. It was a huge moment of growth, and I will always be grateful for attracting situations that allow me to grow.

23

I had done a lot of growing up since the day that final dissertation was handed in. Finally, to my parents' delight, I had thrown myself into the working world during my final year of uni. My thinking was I had better complete my studies away from Teesside, and I moved back home to Kingston upon Hull with my parents. It was never my intention to remain there long: I had big plans, starting with nine months in the United States—North Carolina to be exact. I am still close with many of the families I stayed with to this day; they will always be close to my heart, and my time out in the States was a true transitional experience into adulthood. During the stint, I planned profusely and had implemented my strategy for certain and instant success almost as soon as the Boeing 737 touched down in Manchester Airport. In fact, I made calls to leisure centers, schools, and nurseries prior to coming back. It was in a local business competition where I found my next source of *Aspiration* and the desire to become the next "overnight success," the goal of any young aspiring entrepreneur:

Enter to see if your business is in with a chance for investment from the biggest businessmen and women in Hull and East Yorkshire.

My moment had arrived. I paced up and down the living room of my home, just itching to pick up the phone and find out more information. "Jon Tucker Soccer Schools" was doing fine and picking up a steady bit of business, so I didn't *need* to, but...

"But this is different, Jon," I told myself, "This is your chance."

The man in the photograph stood proud, almost like an Action Man doll in a box fixated into a mold prior to opening. He had this smug look washed across his face, but his watch... wow, the watch. The face glistened a golden tint that screamed success; it was a symbol of accomplishment, one that looked so effortless to the wearer but felt almost out of reach to the rest of us mortals. It appealed heavily to the materialistic nature of a young twenty-something, and my thoughts wandered away with the dopamine effects of visualizing my own success. It wasn't necessarily the item itself; the watch was collateral to winning in life. His definition of winning was money, watches, cars, and suits. From the perspective of somebody who had never possessed that, I was enticed deeper to this particular *Aspiration*. I was already living in a dream where I was the new Action Man.

After contemplating how I would, in turn, spend my first big dividend, I decided to enter the competition. My first face-to-face encounter with Action Man was overwhelming. For those UK readers, it was literally like the TV show *Dragon's Den*. A contestant would pitch an idea to a group of "Dragons" at the front of the room, all facing the nervous contestant with their cash stacked up to showcase their wealth. Trembling with every shuffling step across the room, I handed my flyers to each of the investors. Action Man was particularly intriguing, and he flooded me with questions about my experience and vision. Before I even finished the pitch, he halted me as if to ensure everyone's eyes were on him. Then it came, the news I still to this day couldn't compute as good or bad...

Low and behold, good old Action Man himself decided to invest in my company. At the time, all I could think about was five, ten, even fifteen years down the line, proudly reflecting on all of the success that was bound to come my way. What brought me back down to Earth was his arrogance: reminding everyone who owns the room (both metaphorically and also literally, I was to find out later on!).

He even made a passing comment as he exited, "The name... Jon Tucker... that's from the film, isn't it? We must change it... it's not like David Beckham, is it? Let's be honest... I'll have a think."

I'd not heard that before.

My admiration for Action Man was certainly not for his personality. Similarly to the chief of the football team, his personality left a lot to be desired. It was the way he carried himself, the car he drove, the suit, the watch, the lifestyle. He just seemed so... happy.

I wanted that.

Without hesitation, I accepted the deal and told my family the exciting news: I had won investment and at the age of twenty-three could call myself a business owner!

With *Aspirations,* you can sometimes second-guess yourself. This is slightly different from the *Realization* phase we will get to next. *Aspirations* are often gut feelings or limiting beliefs. I had both a limiting belief I couldn't handle the responsibility of running the company and then the gut feeling something wasn't right. I was a 49 percent shareholder in my own coaching business idea—the other 51 percent belonged to Dan (Action Man), whom I'd met five minutes ago. It also now had his name instead of mine despite his highest qualification for the name of a football company being the fact he'd played for Mansfield Town under 14s. It wasn't exactly "David Beckham," either.

I know what you're thinking: this is what admiration entails. You want something so badly you are prepared to take the hand that appears to be offering you support. You also want to get from A to B in a linear and accelerated manner—which we all know is never how it works out.

Still, all I could think was, "Maybe this is it. Maybe this is my big break."

You see success stories all the time about "overnight millionaires" who started with nothing but an idea and succeeded. Despite my feelings of discomfort, I had a decision to make: embrace the fear of failure in the pursuit of my dream-self or become engulfed by the fear of remaining average. As you age and become wiser, you soon realize this is not actually the case. The majority of success stories appear to be overnight, but nothing suddenly just "happens." One of my favorite books, *Atomic Habits* by James Clear, states:

"Whenever you see an overnight success, your eyes deceive you. What you are witnessing is the hour of opportunity unleashing

the potential energy of previous choices. It was not one decision but the accumulated power of all that came before. The fuse was lit on a loaded cannon."

Every single day: a relentless pursuit of excellence that is consistent over time. Although my area of career interest was saturated with sports providers, I was twenty-three years old and had a whole career ahead of me. I had discovered a range of coaching techniques in the United States, in addition to observing closely the behind-the-scenes running of a successful coaching business to figure out what would and wouldn't work back in the UK.

I decided I was ready to make a go of this and stand shoulder-to-shoulder with Action Man with my Rolex glistening brightly next to his. In the pursuit of my *Aspirations* of becoming a business owner, I set my worries aside and started working for myself the very next day.

26

Each step seemed to echo even louder in the silence of the school corridors than the last. I was full term into my teacher training, and the deputy headteacher at the time, Mike, had only just finished delivering feedback on a lesson he had observed. The words were all extremely positive, and I felt there was potentially an upcoming decision to be made whether I would remain at this place of work permanently or go back to my previous school. The promise of a pathway to success drew me away from my business (among other reasons which I'll delve into later). My loyalties at the time had been with the school that initially offered me a teacher training contract, leading to me closing my coaching business and enrolling in my teacher training course. They had also handed me a job offer postgraduation prior to my placement at the school I was currently scampering through. My destination, and possibly my destiny was here: the boss's office.

"Jon, we think you are fantastic and want to offer you a job for next year."

Straight to the point: I was pretty taken aback. It had only been a matter of weeks that I'd spent at this school. The decision I thought had to be made was whether I would remain in that year group or gain experience elsewhere in the school—but they'd already seen enough! It wasn't even Christmas time yet, and I had two job offers! This was extremely fortunate as some trainees spent the entire year at schools without a single offer, so I was careful to express my gratitude.

"I appreciate the offer. However, I need to think about the other school and—"

"I knew they would've already offered you something, so I want you to let me know what your thoughts are on this…"

The boss began to sell me the dream: subject leadership, pathways to the leadership team—the world was my oyster, and I could go as far as I wanted up the ladder. I thought back to Action Man and his presence in a room; the boss had a similar tone. There was a theme among these leaders, different in many ways to the university figureheads in twenty-one.

"Okay. This sounds like it would be the perfect opportunity to develop my career forward..."

I was right.

"... I'm going to really enjoy working here, thank you."

I was wrong.

My *Aspiration* came from wanting to work at this school, but particularly work for Mike, who mentored me throughout my first four weeks at the new school. He showed me the ropes in teaching and really brought me forward from being an average trainee to a reasonably successful one (though I still doubted myself). His tonality, body language, values, and the fact he visibly cared for the children at his school made him the polar opposite of Action Man. He seemed very internally driven, and he thought of others before himself, not himself before others. He ended up leaving for reasons I'd soon come to understand, but at the same time, it sparked a new *Aspiration: I could be the next Mike.* I could be a leader. This began a new *Purpose Cycle*, my third clear cycle I can recall in my lifetime. This cycle, I knew, would be the one the others had set me up for in the years gone by.

Walking out of the meeting, I felt like I had the world at my feet. Not like I had "made it," like my twenty-three-year-old self, but in a way that sparked true optimism, motivation, and *Aspiration*. I was prepared to do what it took to make myself a success. For the rest of my time on my training placement I went the extra mile. I sat to have lunch with the kids from other classes to get to know everyone in the school. I spoke to the cleaners to learn their names and about their families. I covered various extracurricular clubs and even researched ideas that would help drive the school forward. I was developing an obsession for success, but this time it felt like it was for something meaningful. My work felt like it had *Purpose.*

Each of the cycles you have seen across the three timelines have outlined some form of *Aspiration.* My *Aspiration* came from seeing other people in places where I wanted to be— or didn't want to be in some cases. As you delve into the steps, you will see how I have found a way to make a step up through each cycle to aspire to greater *Purposes* and also more meaningful *Purposes.* This will come hand-in-hand alongside finding your true *Purpose*—or your "why," as Simon Sinek would say (Sinek, 2011). The importance of each cycle is you learn from each phase and each cycle.

The High Performance Podcast is an incredible podcast by Humphrey and Hughes in which Sir Clive Woodward stated the three elements of implementing high performance, "Discover, Distill, Do." I believe this is highly relevant for reflecting on past cycles.

First, you gather a range of information about a subject or situation

Then you distill the information into relevance and key points to help you grow.

Finally, you action those steps and become a better you when implementing the next *Purpose Cycle.* What you will find is as you start to contextualize the areas of your life you want to develop, you will build the successful blocks toward achieving *Purpose*, similar to Maslow and his hierarchy of needs.

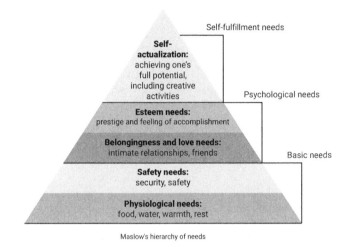

Maslow's hierarchy of needs

Figure 4—Maslow and his hierarchy of needs as explained in *Psychological Review* in 1943.

My take on this is the need of *Self-Actualization* is the overall feeling of *Purpose*. The piece that is missing in many people's lives. The intangible aspect of one's life that once they find, they become complete. Many may never know what is missing until they find *Purpose*. Others search their whole lives for it. In the next section, I break down the key components of *Aspiration*.

CHAPTER 2

Finding *Aspiration*

———

Aspiration varies at different ages. It can begin with a simple car driving past you on the high street and you thinking, *Wow! I'd love to drive a car like that someday,* or an Instagram post from an influencer that depicts the "perfect life." This is the initial step in what I call the *Purpose Cycle.* *Aspiration* triggers an actuating of feelings that give you an initial drive—like a shot of adrenaline or, for some, a liter of high-caffeine energy drink. For other people, it is envy or jealousy. Most of us will experience one extreme or the other: toxicity or momentum—there is rarely an in-between. This step could have also been called "admiration" or "adoration," but this is solely down to the stage you are at in your life right now. What is tangible, veracious *Aspiration,* and what is an imposturous, "Petrarchan lover" of admiration that will consume any self-confidence you uphold?

I want you to think back to all of the times in your past you have admired, envied, commended, desired, respected, craved, idolized, or even begrudged others. Why did you feel like this? Interestingly enough, when we are young, admiration exists only in innocence.

"I want to score the winning goal at Wembley," one child might say.

"I dream of performing in the Royal Ballet as the main role," says another.

Where does this innocence go? Why do our dreams shape toward admiration for a figure in the bank or a particular-looking partner? Is this *really* what is going to make you happy? What many people discover is these *Aspirations* burn out. *Aspiration* is finite; it gets you in the vehicle toward success. *Motivation* is the ignition that starts the engine. In this metaphor of life, you will need *discipline* as the fuel to continue to show up and be consistent day in, day out. This will come in the later chapter, "*Inspiration.*" But as you begin your most important *Purpose Cycle* to date, it is important you picture your final step so you understand what it will take to get there, and how it will feel to be there. You now have the control to shape the outcome you desire the most. You are now tapping into your "greater self." It's a kind of *red pill* moment if you will, in reference to *The Matrix*. So, let's go down the rabbit hole of personal development.

The key to begin is to find and develop an *Aspiration*. This could be formed by knowing what it is you want, or on the other hand, knowing exactly what you don't want! This idea could be formed by triumph or trauma. You could see somebody win a fitness challenge, or you could experience what it feels like to lose.

In my first ever cross-country race, I came dead last (by a long, long way, too). My *Aspiration* changed from wanting a hobby to not wanting to come last ever again. It filled me with a relentless desire to train to my potential each session. Once I had won my first race, my *Aspiration* changed again. It became addictive to win, and I had to replicate that feeling. I never got sick of finishing first, and that became the new *Aspiration*.

Aspiration comes before *Inspiration* nearly all of the time. This is because you often witness, hear about, or read about events that can trigger that internal feeling. It's the initial viewpoint of seeing that for yourself before wanting to follow suit. This is why younger people often see glory-based results such as winning a competition or excelling in an activity as something they would like to do too. The mirror neurons in our brain associate what others do as a desirable path to follow. Mirror neurons were first discovered in research on monkeys, where they saw peers complete an action and wanted to copy. The mirror neurons in their brains were active just as much when they were watching their peers as they were when they were actually doing the action (Kilner and Lemon, 2013).

This is where the phrase "Monkey see, monkey do" comes from. When we witness a perceived *Aspiration*, our mirror neurons signal to us the feelings of doing those actions ourselves. Whereas as we get older, our *Aspirations* change and they become much more tangible goals based on our experiences and our internal beliefs shaped by our upbringing and environment.

Your initial preparation for the journey ahead is to think about *exactly* what you want from *The Purpose Cycle*. Get out a pencil and a notepad and write down three goals if you want to. I will be setting a range of tasks for you to accomplish throughout this book because while I take you through my journey, I will be taking you on yours. Let's be clear here: you are reading this because you're as much of a fan of personal development as I am. If you feel like you are at rock bottom, trust me, you're not.

The devastating characteristic that clouds over those at rock bottom is one that is of being blissfully unaware—until, quite often, your decisions and ignorance to the signals life is giving you is too far gone. If you are reading this and you have made a conscious effort to turn your life around, then I applaud you because you have already accomplished the most difficult obstacle of beginning your *Purpose Cycle*. Some of you reading this may already be quite deep in your *Purpose Cycle* and will identify with a particular step further down the line. You will know this because you will be aware of a time where you began one step and subsequently left the next. The first thing we need to let go of is the limiting beliefs that have held you back in the past.

LIMITING BELIEFS

A limiting belief is the idea of a certain worldview being the absolute truth. This could range from "I never seem to have any luck in my life" to "I always ruin job interviews for myself due to my nerves."

If there is one thing that defeats a person before they even start, it is the voice in their heads telling them they can't do it. Some of the thoughts I had before writing this book were:

"What if my friends tell me I'm being utterly ridiculous?"

"I don't have the time to execute my plans."

"But... what if I fail?"

It is natural for anyone to project the worst-case scenario; the difference between an optimist and a pessimist is that a pessimist takes note of these thoughts and creates a limiting belief. These types of thoughts can prove to be detrimental long-term. The worst way of dealing with these thoughts is to discard them.

"Avoiding your emotions and positive thinking are two very different things. Once you learn to face and accept your emotions, you can rewrite your limiting beliefs—and then, positive responses will develop more naturally."

—VEX KING

I took a lot from these words when I first read them. I always thought I was dealing with my limiting beliefs by discarding them to the back of my mind—unbeknown to me, these negative thoughts were being stowed away until a pressure situation arose. Then they were heightened, ten times worse!

Limiting beliefs are what often stall people before they have even started. They play out scenarios in their head that are simply not true but are based on the worst possible case or are exaggerated based on previous experiences. For example, a child may not want to try riding a bike again because the last time they got on a bike, they fell. Even though the pain was a temporary feeling, they remember how that made them feel and subsequently refuse to get back on a bike because they feel like they will get hurt again, and maybe even worse than the last time.

If you've ever been knocked back for a promotion or applied for a course you didn't get on at university, you may have had this type of mindset before. Heck, I applied for dozens of jobs during my early twenties and got knocked back countless times! Trying to get in at entry-level while being told "you need experience" is demoralizing, but the longer you let these beliefs manifest, the harder it is going to be to overcome them. Instead, dream up your *Aspiration* and enjoy the process of possible rejection. Think to yourself, "If it was easy to attain my dream, then everyone would have it. I am brave and unique because I dare to dream bigger." Positive affirmations are some of the best ways to overcome limiting beliefs because you are embedding new beliefs into your thinking.

This is the same for adults who struggle to give people a chance when building relationships. They will base judgment upon a previous experience. Somebody who is unemployed may fear applying for a job due to the fear of rejection. If a person has lost money investing, they refuse to try again due to the potential losses they can incur again. The key to all three of these (and other limiting beliefs) is to reflect on the situation, look at the lessons the universe was trying to teach us, and learn before trying again.

Do limiting beliefs sound familiar? We need to change a key relationship in your life.

THE MOST IMPORTANT RELATIONSHIP YOU'LL EVER HAVE

Self-love is defined as regard for one's own well-being and happiness (Oxford English Dictionary, 2004).

There is a reason why you receive the preflight instructions on a plane to apply your own oxygen mask before helping others: if you are "on empty" yourself, then you are in no position to care for others. Working on yourself for this journey is essential for *Fruition*. Another way of understanding this analogy is you shouldn't expect other people to use their oxygen masks for you. Your growth is your own responsibility, and you should expect the people around you to be focusing on their own personal growth.

In Vex King's *Good Vibes, Good Life*, he speaks about self-love in a way that resonates with me each day. He speaks about the unconditional love we have for others. So, self-love must also show that same love toward us. This doesn't mean we allow ourselves to remain unchallenged by unreasonable behavior; we hold ourselves accountable but appreciate where we are at our stage of growth. As King states, "Self-Love is the balance between accepting yourself as you are while knowing you deserve better and working toward it."

A way of dictating your self-love is to change your mindset on your self-talk. By doing this, you will find yourself challenging your limiting beliefs, therefore proving to yourself you are capable of exceeding your expectations!

SELF-TALK

In the world where we currently live, it becomes increasingly important to recognize the value you have. Before you love others, you need to be comfortable with yourself. Self-talk is a huge part of this because what you say (internally by thinking or externally by speaking) has an effect on your own happiness. You need to prioritize your language and encourage that voice in your head to speak in a positive manner. The conversations you have with your peers are forms of communication that can either build positive or negative emotions. The majority of the time, we choose to speak in a manner that has positive implications—because that's how we are socially programmed. We understand the consequences of our words. So why do we choose to degrade ourselves with our self-talk? If you want to delve into this further, there is an affirmation exercise on my website called "The Self-Talk Week."

BEING SELFISH

At times you will have to look after yourself. Many perceive this as being selfish, but if you tend to take on a lot for the sake of others, you may be neglecting your own needs in the process. This is where you must find time to be "selfish" and recharge your own battery so you can be there for others again. You need to understand that "no" is an acceptable answer at times.

Especially say "no" if those people who need you the most drain your energy because of the sheer amount of effort you put in to ensure their happiness prioritizes over yours. This sounds like a horrible thing to say, but it is just honesty. There are people who are going through tough times or dramas, and that does exert a lot of mental energy to pick them up. To be at your optimum, you must look after yourself first. This could be something as simple as running yourself a bath, reading a book, taking a yoga class, or even switching your phone off from the world around you.

Dedicate yourself to at least one hour of "you" time a day to fulfill your own happiness and be ready to help others the next day. Making yourself a priority every once in a while is not selfish. It's necessary.

CHOOSE THE LONG-TERM "YOU"

Self-love isn't about making the immediate choices that suit you at the time because it is "easier." You may have had points in life where you had to give friends or family "tough love," such as telling a friend their partner is acting in a toxic manner in their relationship, removing a valued possession from your child, or even not speaking to someone until their actions change. This is usually because you can see they are not being true to their identity, or they are self-sabotaging their identity or beliefs. To act in accordance with your future self, understand what characteristics your ideal "you" have, what beliefs and identities they have, and reflect on how you are acting now. What is it you need to change?

Thinking long-term helps with this. If you want to lose weight and you look outside to see the pouring rain, your first thought could be to remain warm and dry indoors and skip the run that night. That is a natural feeling. After all, you aren't going to lose half a stone from one run, nor are you going to put on half a stone if you miss a run. The problem that lies within this thought pattern is you are not acting in accordance with your future self, the one who is disciplined and has already shifted a stone in weight by running regularly because they are committed to their goals. Those are the beliefs of the long-term/future you. All decisions in life are compounded, just like how financial interest compounds over time in a positive or negative manner (debt vs. investments). Ensure you are investing in yourself rather than getting into emotional debt.

Whenever you are faced with that dilemma, choose the future "you," rather than the comfort zone/dissatisfied version of you who wanted to make a change in the first place. It is equally as important to be realistic in your goals. You may have to adjust your path every once in a while. You won't make every 5:00 a.m. gym session, but what are you going to do about it? Go at 5:00 p.m. when you have a spare half an hour. The worst workout is the one you didn't do.

Make changes, not excuses. We all possess the most valuable currency of all: time. We get to choose how we spend it, and just like my other money-related analogies, many people waste it, and few choose to invest and spend wisely.

SELF-SIGNALING AND SELF-CONTROL
Self-signaling is the art of pointing yourself toward a specific goal—the phrase "fake it 'til you make it" can be interpreted to have negative connotations in this scenario. You need to live within your means while directing yourself toward where you want to go. To do this, you need to show self-control. This

will provide the signals to show you that you're on the right path when developing an *Aspiration*.

According to Prelec and Bodner in a 2003 article named "Self-Signaling and Self-Control":

"Self-control is a hallmark virtue of human character. To lack self-control is to be governed by momentary pleasures even when these pleasures place larger values at risk. Willing the tired body to exercise or the tired mind to another hour of work are but two examples of active self-control—the tolerance of pain in return for a larger but more remote and uncertain gain. Turning down a chocolate dessert or an attractive sexual encounter are examples of passive self-control—avoiding immediate gratification in order to preserve broader personal objectives or self-esteem."

This explains why practicing active self-control is so much more difficult than passive self-control. Saying "no" to something is much simpler than saying "yes." We should actually recognize the hundreds of decisions each day as opportunities to celebrate progress and think consciously about how often you make active and passive self-control decisions. People who take on challenges like "Stoptober" (cutting out drinking or smoking for the month of October) or "Veganuary" (cutting out meat and other animal-based produce for the month of January) find they become pretty successful for two reasons: 1) They have to basically say "no" for a month and 2) They know it won't be forever. Once a habit is formed, people are much more open to making permanent changes when they realize how easy passive self-control is. Forty percent of Veganuary participants were planning on remaining vegan once they had completed their initial month (Starostinetskaya, 2021). This prompted my thinking, why don't we make all choices passive by flipping our mindset?

Instead of the active self-control of "I have to get out of bed to exercise" and saying "yes" to it, why don't you pass on "I choose to remain in my average zone, unhappy and far away from my goals." That way, you say "no" to that life and make positive steps forward. Switch up your thinking if faced with the difficulty of forming a habit. Even set yourself a month-long challenge like the ones above.

BEING KIND

Although time is a currency we can never truly earn back, kindness is the opposite. The more you give, the more you receive. Self-improvement is about radiating good feelings, and although we never give to receive, we must understand the physiological and psychological benefits that come along with kindness. When you help somebody, you begin to accumulate nuggets of joy that put a spring in your step. These acts of kindness don't necessarily have to cost you money, and it also doesn't matter if a person knows the identity of their benefactor of kindness. All that matters is you make somebody else's day better. Who knows, maybe it's true that what goes around, comes around, and you will receive the infectious effects of kindness from somebody else in your community.

Once you begin to celebrate the victories of other people, rather than feel the bitterness and anger associated with jealousy, then you can be assured you're on a journey of self-actualization—becoming at peace with yourself.

To summarize, *Aspiration* is the drive that begins this journey. Many of us can be shocked into an *Aspiration* about what we *do* want. Other times, we can see in plain sight what we *don't want*. An important way to approach this stage is to develop a relationship with yourself so that your mindset is correct. This becomes the foundation to any *Purpose Cycle*—and future cycles, too. How you treat yourself will project onto others, and you will naturally begin to attract more opportunities and positive experiences. To help us cultivate this mindset, I have devised a series of tasks for you to undertake in the next chapter.

CHAPTER 3

Tasks

TASK 1—POSITIVE SELF-TALK

VICTORIES

First, draw a table on a page and write down *twenty* victories you have had over the past year. No matter how much you believe they are insignificant, write them down. Make each victory clear and specific. For example, "having children" is not what I am looking for, but "raising two beautiful and happy children" is more on the lines of what we are after. Become specific in your victories because we will be going specific into your *Aspirations*. To "become rich" is a broad, throwaway desire that has no real substance to it. The specific goal would be, "I want to become financially free by developing multiple revenue streams that allow my finances to grow automatically." The more attention we pay to ourselves, the more we will notice about ourselves. We often nitpick potential dating partners, job opportunities, or even large purchases such as houses and cars, so let's be specific with the most important thing—*you*.

My Victories				

Struggled to fill them up? You need to give yourself more credit for your accomplishments and victories. Have you helped an elderly lady cross the street? Have you made your bed this morning? Have you decided to walk to the shops rather than drive? All of these can be perceived as victories!

Now, if you *still* can't fill up the list, what are you waiting for? Be proactive. Go and win! Donate to a charity, be generous to a random person, or leave a tip for the young barista who asked how your day was. Despite these seeming minuscule to you, they are building momentum for what is about to come. We are on a journey together to first change your perception and then channel your *Aspiration* positively.

Now I want you to order your victories in order of importance to *you*. What do you perceive as your "biggest" victory?

Has your victory impacted positively on somebody else's life? Does it help you grow closer to your goals? Note them in order and study the results. Do you find yourself top-heavy with large accomplishments from your life so far? What we are going to work on is balancing those out with more and more tiny victories each day. Workout in the morning? There's one! Got to work early? Another! Made the deadline for that paperwork? See what we're doing here? Recognizing our accomplishments builds a more positive outlook with which to view life.

From this page onward, your viewpoint on your environment will be from a frame of positivity. You have proven to yourself you achieve something every week! If you ever need to remind yourself of this, repeat this task on paper. Each day has numerous victories. I want you to gather up in your memories like a squirrel gathering acorns—but fear not if one of those acorns don't come your way. Each perceived failure is welcomed as an opportunity to learn. As Ant Middleton states in *The Fear Bubble,* "Failure is allowing the mistake to win."

Developing *Aspiration* will begin to form as you gather a momentum of victories. The casual dopamine hit of a good deed will signal to your psyche you enjoy certain victories more than others, and you will in turn want to pursue more. What years of reading personal development books have taught me is once you begin to live with an abundance mindset, doors begin to open. An *Aspiration* for a greater life is a pursuit that should enthrall everybody, but sadly, you may believe this isn't for the masses. If so, wouldn't everybody have what Ramit Sethi calls a *"Rich Life"* (Ramit Sethi, 2009)?

Let me break that barrier down straight away. *You can* have a rich life as can everybody. The secret? Consistency in manifestation and action. I call a "rich life" something slightly different: *Fruition*. This is due to a belief I have instilled over a number of years by studying the absolute high performers in life. *Fruition* is a product of correct manifestation and action. Once you reach *Fruition*, you can then begin your cycle again and aspire further. Hence the name, *The Purpose Cycle*. Look at the victories you have already achieved. Now write down twenty victories that the future, high performing you will be achieving following this journey. This is you living your rich life. To live it, you need to see it first.

Now that your self-talk has been reframed let the manifestation commence. Think back to what you have aspired to previously. Is this still the case? What does your future contain? It is time for exercise number two.

TASK 2—MANIFESTATION EXERCISE PART 1—VISION BOARD

This exercise is common among those who are interested in the Law of Attraction, but for those who may not be familiar, this exercise alone was single-handedly the most important thing I did on my third major *Purpose Cycle* leading to this book. A vision board is a physical and visual way of manifesting your goals. To be able to consciously and subconsciously see your dreams each day is powerful.

To visualize your goal each day attracts it to your life like gravity. It also assists the power of your thoughts, feelings, and actions.

You grow fond of your future self by feeling the chemical effects internally of what it would be like to succeed—hence the term "Positive Affirmation." The life you desire is attainable. You may just need to see it first.

As my fiancée and I sat down with a glass of "19 Crimes" red in hand, we spoke in-depth about what we wanted once we were married. At that stage, we felt like there was no point in implementing anything now toward our goals because all of our savings were dedicated toward the wedding. We had the classic idea of setting up a wedding Pinterest page and accumulated funds each month steadily. Many months elapsed, and we managed to chip away at the total wedding cost each month.

During this conversation, something amazing happened: we began to think hypothetically, "What would our marital home look like?"

"Where do you want to live?"

"Would you want an office/study room in the house?"

"New build or renovation?"

Once we began delving deeper and deeper into the idea of owning a home, the dopamine release of anticipation—the one you get when you see a chocolate bar or test-drive a new car—diffused into our system. We both had a feeling of excitement and elation about the possibility of owning a home together instead of renting. My partner, Sarah, said to me, "We have a cork board upstairs we don't use. Go and bring it down, and we can create a vision board."

Having not thought of this myself, I was first of all skeptical, "I don't want us to get our hopes up. There's no way we can possibly afford a house before we get married."

Sarah encouraged me to be open-minded and put a halt to the pessimism disrupting our Saturday night, and I dashed upstairs to retrieve the key to our *Aspirations*.

Over the next couple of hours, we scoured the internet for photographs of our dream items for each room of our fictional home. Every detail was covered, including the oak entrance porch welcoming guests to our home and the dressing room for Sarah. Once complete, our vision board took pride in place directly opposite our bed, so each morning, we would wake up and see it, even if it was subconscious at times. Without realizing it, we were manifesting our goals. I was acting in accordance to one day reaching these goals. Everything I was doing was centered around living the life I strove for. The subconscious element of seeing them but not consciously noticing them helped transition our daily behaviors from "motivated" to "disciplined."

I've always believed motivation comes and goes, but discipline is really what drives you to your goals. As I stated earlier with the metaphor of the vehicle moving toward your goals: *Aspiration* unlocks the door, motivation is the ignition, and discipline is the fuel that will take you there.

I want you to find a vision board. I would suggest making a physical one like we did. Either buy one or create one using a spare wall, sheet of paper, or anything that can resemble a real-life Pinterest board! Then print the photos of what you want to achieve (remember to be specific). Then place the vision board somewhere in your house that you will see every day. My suggestion would be the bedroom, that way you'll see it every morning when you wake up, and every night when you go to sleep.

It took us over thirty months to save for a wedding, but only ten to save for a deposit for our first home. It was by no means a cheap home either. We went from renting a two up, two down home in the town center to a suburban new build with four bedrooms and a garage. The dream house on the vision board wasn't the same as the house we bought, but this is the first step to that ultimate vision. With the photographs being pinned on the board, the final vision may alter as we grow older. The point of the exercise is to make your *Aspirations* a part of your identity and familiarize yourself with them each and every day—even if it is subconsciously. The world works in a way in which it will begin to open doors, albeit a-jar, where you are able to see your *Aspirations* and can openly pursue them.

TASK 3—MANIFESTATION EXERCISE PART 2
I want you to repeat this exercise as many times as you need to for your goals to become clear in your head:

Picture yourself in a cinema. You may have people in the theater with you, or you may not. The film comes on and it is you. It shows your small wins turn into opportunities, which in turn, prospers into large victories, which lead to *Fruition*. Who is around you? Who is *truly* cheering for you? Interesting, isn't it?

The film begins to cut back at speed to the past. You see a younger self at the beginning of this cycle, but in what you thought was the *Aspiration* phase, it was actually the *Admiration* for something more materialistic or avaricious. Can you realize now why this was the case? Were your motives all wrong or not aligned? How will this influence your future self in your pursuit of *Fruition*? You keep fast-forwarding this part of the film, then rewinding it back, then forward, then back—so much so the film actually burns up! A new film needs inserting into the projector.

This new film is blank. You are the director. Picture *Fruition*. What does this look like? Who is around you? Where is this? How did you achieve this? Every trait you want in your future version of you is being demonstrated in this film. You are overcoming every single challenge. Look at the confidence you radiate and the way you are self-assured as you handle every piece of criticism or doubt your way. You are achieving *Fruition,* and those feelings you can feel while watching the film are the feelings you will feel again. The feeling is so great you want more of it. As the film ends, you want to turn it into reality, which it is. All you have to do is act in accordance with the version of you that you just watched in the film.

Look around at the audience in the cinema and stand up to face them. How are they reacting? Take a bow and be proud of your future achievements. Because here is your first step of *Aspiration*, and you have now realized it.

CHANNELING ASPIRATION

You must approach your goals with a huge amount of optimism and think "why not" rather than "why." Optimism is about the future. It is not blind positivity, nor is it naive. It is not seeing the glass as half full and ignoring the half of glass that is empty. It is the ability to see the emptiness of half the glass while choosing to focus on the fullness of the other half. See the shining light in the face of adversity. When most people dream of a goal, they always think of the problems that could occur when they get started: "I could get into debt," "People might laugh at me," "What if nobody buys my book?"

These dream killing ideas are the reasons why most people remain ordinary. An idea remains a pipe dream and that's all it is. I've experienced this at close hand within my own family, and it is a mindset ingrained into us by our close circles from an early age. It is always comfortable to play it safe, right? What we need to do is break past that stereotypical view of dreams and actually turn them into reality. Be open-minded, of course. You will undoubtedly face challenges along the way, and that's why only a small percentage of people actually pursue their dreams successfully, but you have to be optimistic. If you can't believe in yourself, then who will?

Putting it nicely, for as long as you are personally developing yourself for other people, you will never achieve true *Fruition*. You will always be chasing the pot of gold at the end of the rainbow. Trust me, that pot never gets found. It's also important to remember the side-effects of personal development usually rub off on others anyway, so by becoming a better you, your children will notice the positive change, as will your partner or a coworker.

This is why your *Aspiration* needs to be personal. What is it that you want? Why do you want it? What will *you* do to make sure you get there? How will you ensure your goal will come to *Fruition*? If you are not taking personal responsibility for each step of the *Purpose Cycle*—whether you complete it or not—then you will never ultimately find *Fruition*. Don't get me wrong. There are always difficulties, hence the next step: *Realization*. This next phase is when the obstacles appear, and 90 percent of people either hide away, give up, or claim "luck just wasn't on my side."

LESSONS LEARNED FROM *ASPIRATION*:

1. It is great to see a perceived end goal or finished article, but in reality, it may not be what you actually want. There's a phrase which states, "never meet your heroes" because your perception of them is the frame of what they want you to see. So, it is important to aspire to something that isn't superficial, fake, or something you're not exactly familiar with. **Look at the entire goal and decide if it is something you want to pursue.**

2. If you never actually aspire toward a goal, then you will never get there. You can't just aspire to "have money." You must understand what it is you want and why you want it. Is this going to make you a better version of yourself? Is it going to improve the quality of your life? **Make your *Aspiration* a part of your identity and own it.**

3. **Visualization is an excellent way to map out your goals.**
   It enables you to see the finish line and the necessary
   steps to get there. As a whole, you will visualize more of
   the positive scenarios associated with the end goal. The
   next chapter will show you how to deal with the more
   challenging aspects of your goal.

Three lessons I've learned about myself during my own
Aspiration *stage:*

1.

2.

3.

Key Character trait: **Optimism**

PART 2

REALIZATION

CHAPTER 4

Awakening

21

It took only six minutes between disembarking from the hell that was a thirty-six-hour coach journey and a representative from our coach making a fool of themselves—if they hadn't done so already. In truth, the awakening took place midjourney during the confrontation with Mark when I eventually realized the company I kept wasn't exactly my cup of tea. I had always conformed to social rules—wanting to be a part of the university circus and be accepted. *Realization* is a true awakening and awareness of oneself. My first experience with it was when I figured out my old *Aspirations* were not what I really valued in life. In the past, status among a social circle was extremely important to me. Upon observing Mark's behavior, I saw a dynamic I didn't want to be a part of. My close friend, Anthony, noticed my discomfort.

"You okay, mate?"

"Yeah, great..."

It seemed evident to the attentive eye I was still reluctant to open up to one of my best mates. After all, it was in this very social setting of a university football club that we met, so would he just think I was a fraud?

Admittedly, I did *still* want acceptance, but to not pay the price this particular social circle was demanding. Given the situation I was in, ostracizing myself miles away from the solitude of home wouldn't be the smartest move. I decided to keep my head down and see the week out. After all, *Situational Realization* is often about reading the room. You may not want to be there, but a swift escape is not always possible. I've worked jobs before and had the realization I didn't want to work there anymore, but you can't exactly announce you are quitting and abscond like you see folks do in the movies. Patience often pays off.

Thankfully, I was rooming with a pair of nervous freshmen. They were probably as equally grateful they drew my name out of the hat as their "senior." My instructions were simple: give them challenges throughout the tour and make it as uncomfortable as possible. Some seniors took this literally and made their freshers sleep in the bath, or worse, threw their mattress out of the hotel (causing the room to wave "goodbye" to their security deposit).

Newly awakened, I realized these wide-eyed, fresh-faced lads probably saw Mark's behavior on the coach and either: a) prayed they didn't draw his name, or b) potentially envisioned their place at the head of the coach on next year's tour already.

Their own *Aspiration* stage began, and it pained me to see some of the guys idolizing the behavior with their priorities mixed up. Some leaders rule through fear. I assessed the faces of these younger men, and it was evident (like so many in their late teens) their *Aspirations* are closely linked to their social standing. Sadly, many young people center their *Aspirations* around their peers and put the "alphas" on a pedestal. This step in my journey was a huge turning point. The realization that showed me seeking gratification from other people was never going to make me truly happy. I now had to show these two freshmen it wasn't going to make them happy either.

Two names were drawn out with mine. They grabbed their luggage and walked with me to our room for the week. My instructions to the two lads were simple, but my goal for the week even more so: demonstrate to the two freshmen that to enjoy this trip, you don't have to drink urine, throw beer across balconies, or run naked down the streets of Salou. This situation didn't have to be one that resembled what I had experienced on the coach.

"Right lads, before we get ready to meet in the first bar, I just want you all to know I won't be doing any of this stuff you heard pretour. Just enjoy the trip. We'll all stay out of trouble with the other universities, and don't let any of the other freshers or seniors in our room. The 'banter' can take place elsewhere," I said.

Throughout the four-day binge in Spain, I managed to find some quiet time where I could reflect. Now I knew what I didn't want, and I needed to work out what I did want. The sooner I got back, the better. I counted the days, hours, and minutes tenaciously. This lifestyle of drinking obsessively, making fools of ourselves, and trying to win over the praise of the pack wasn't part of my identity. The worst part is, until reading this book, many of my best friends would have still thought I enjoyed that lifestyle. Don't get me wrong, I enjoyed the camaraderie of the team during football games, the spirit centered around the sport itself, and building a bond relating to our success. This trip was something else, though, just like the previous year. I made the most of university life and being young, but I masked my true self in the situations I felt alien in. It was easier to conform with the majority than to be perceived as somebody who was odd or didn't fit in.

Anthony, my closest confidant on the trip, could either sense something was not right with me, or he hated the thought of that prospective return coach journey as much as I did.

"Mate, I've got us two tickets for a flight out of here on the day we check out of the hotel. The rest of the lads will have a thirty-six-hour journey home to endure, and we'll be touching down in the UK before they've even boarded the bus!"

Not all heroes wear capes.

23

A week down the line as a business owner (and one local paper article later), I was enjoying balancing my week with suit-wearing and networking, paired with delivering sports sessions in my recently rebranded coaching attire to the newly branded sports company (I was too thrilled by my success to care my name wasn't on my company). I was enjoying getting my face out there and generating my own work—and I was pretty successful with this too. Despite my income and initial success, I had two concerns.

First, I was struggling to see how I was going to scale up the business as there was actually little-to-no real "investment," just the purchasing of some footballs, cones, and other sporting supplies for my sessions. The second concern was that I had left working as a barista in a coffee shop to become a business owner, but I was receiving no basic pay to keep afloat. I had to arrange a meeting with the other majority shareholder to discuss a basic package that could allow me to grow the business as well as survive. A nervous amble up a winding staircase led me to a door on the top floor of the city center building. I took a deep breath and entered the room.

My "investor" sat hubristically in his large leather chair and spun around as if he were some sort of Bond villain. He must've been expecting me. It was clear from our conversation he just did not live in the same world as me. What I once mistakenly admired as confidence soon became completely the opposite. I have never met a more supercilious man, and the demeanor of his body language and tone had clued me into his personality. My *Realization of Others* had become apparent: this person was going to be a giant obstacle between me and my long-term *Aspirations*.

"Business owners don't see any money until the end of the financial year, Jon," he graciously described.

My amazement continued at how he managed to hold a conversation with me while looking directly through me at the same time. "You're just going to have to get by!"

"Look, I need a basic wage as a coach," I replied.

By this point, he got what he wanted. I was almost begging. "I can't afford to work for free for an entire year. I'll have to get work elsewhere to cover this business, which is why I left serving coffee at Costa!"

"Any work you do for any other company will be for your services, and your services are tied to this company… therefore, you need to invoice them from us," he continued.

I couldn't believe what I was hearing. *Is this some form of modern-day slavery?* I thought to myself. The illusion of Action Man had died off long ago—now he was just "Dan."

A few days later, I still hadn't gotten anywhere with him. I was officially the most broke business owner of all time! I was at the office one day with a meeting lined up with Dan. I had some leads to build the business and try to win over his gratification. Then I received a life-shattering phone call from a friend that would blow this whole problem away but presented something unforeseen and heart-breaking.

"Jon," said Liam, one of my closest friends who called me, as he usually does, but this time it was his birthday and during working hours.

So, it must've been important. His tone was somewhat unexpected of a newly crowned twenty-four-year-old. He seemed... vacant. He called to break the tragic news I can recall so vividly to this day.

"It's Steve... he died last night."

At that exact moment, my life collapsed. I fumbled a pile of flyers I had collected, ready to distribute, completely across the floor. My trembling hands could not grasp a single object by this point, and I could not even muster one comprehensible sound back to him.

"We're all like that, Tucks. I was shocked too when I found out. We are heading to my house to try and process what's happened."

Steve had been a huge part of our group for our school years and remained an integral part of the group whenever we met up during university. He was a straight-A student who had absolutely everything: the charm, the intelligence, the talent. He moved up north to become a teacher in Darlington and developed a rare heart condition at the age of twenty-three. Steve had waited months for a heart transplant, and complications during surgery led to his passing on the thirteenth of October 2014.

The hour after I heard the news, everything took place in slow motion. The wallpaper that littered the walls in the office was a fuzzy blur. I couldn't decipher if it was down to the current whirlwind occupying my brain or if I was holding back the tears so much they had completely flooded my eyes and beclouded every image in sight.

"Where are you going?" echoed Dan, who had clocked my exit as I stumbled unsubtly down the stairs.

By this point, I was fighting every possible emotion a man can feel when one of his closest friends passes away.

"I have to go," I vacantly uttered, "One of my best friends has passed away. I've just found out."

"Oh, Jon… that is awful… I wanted to talk to you about your money," he replied as he turned his back midsentence and began walking.

Was he really doing this? Right now?

The next twenty minutes were a complete blank as I was thinking about my memories of Steve and our last conversation before his passing. His social media was still present. His text messages were still on my phone. I began to deny this had even happened and questioned myself several times while vacantly nodding my head during the meeting, unaware of what was happening in the very room I was sitting in. Between leaving my impromptu meeting with the hero-turned-Bond villain and making my way to Liam's house, my thoughts raced around like the chaos of some form of natural disaster. What had happened in the space of a week is I had the *Realization* this person who I admired and thought would channel my *Aspiration* to become successful was actually toxic. I had never felt so trapped, alone, and deceived in my twenty-three years on this planet.

27

Role models are a funny thing to have. For every "Mike Ross," there's a "Harvey Specter" (for those avid *Suits* viewers out there). The betrayal of who I thought was a mentor four years earlier had made me less able to accept mentorship, guidance, and mutual trust.

At the age of twenty-seven, I was in the first year at my workplace. The atmosphere at the school turned nasty once my mentor, Mike, had left. In his absence, the deputy head, who had been absent during my early days at the school, had returned and seemed to have an agenda against certain people in the school. I was doing my utmost to win her over, going over the top with flowers for Christmas, being overly nice, and making general conversation. Trying to sanitize a negative situation with showers of positivity should work, but it can sometimes work *against* you if that person holds a lot of resentment or anger. This appeared to be one of those times. I used to believe the only way to battle negativity was to flood the situation with positive messages. However, a more neutral, nonreactive approach combined with self-control is all that's needed in times when people are looking for a reaction. Being nice just winds some people up even more!

In the following chapter, I will define the four types of *Realization*. So far, I'd dealt with *Situational Realization* in my university days (where my environment dictated my *Purpose Cycle*) and the *Realization of Others* in my business-owning years. I knew that simply blaming others was not going to work. Although, yes, the environment was toxic, and some of the people certainly didn't want me to succeed, the only way I could come out of this situation in a positive manner was to take ownership of the situation and make it about finding my way through. This was a *Self-Realization*.

As soon as I got home, I laid down on my bed and stared at the ceiling. What were *my* flaws? What did *I* need to improve on to be successful in my career? I made a mental list, then made a written list. I began journaling my days to become more reflective and more efficient. I was struggling with sleep, so I wrote down my thoughts or jobs for the following day on paper, so I didn't have as many thoughts crowding my brain. I watched my fellow trainees, who had also obtained jobs at the school, quitting the profession of teaching altogether. I didn't want to be another casualty of this toxic leadership.

One of my main criticisms was that I was not "open enough emotionally." This was correct. I did tend to withhold emotions, and when the going got tough, I would just try to brush it off and get on with it, just as I had done with my limiting beliefs in the past. I was going through an emotionally draining time as my partner, and I dealt with an ongoing family situation. I felt like this was something to open up to my boss so she could understand there was a crisis going on outside of work. I was optimistic she would see I was finding it tough. In hindsight, I was really not coping well, and my mental health was deteriorating as a result of not balancing the pressures of work and home life. Many people neglect their own needs (think back to Maslow) when these obstacles appear.

I was hoping to gain some advice or even just feel like my superiors understood me so I could feel the weight off my shoulders and get myself back to my optimum self.

What actually happened was quite the opposite.

She reacted to the news by listening without saying much, which I found useful to unload the stress by emoting my thoughts and felt like we'd connected as employer and employee. They say men should open up and talk when they are struggling mentally. However, this seemed to cause further problems for me. I was put on a capability plan, meaning I could potentially lose my job—stating my personal life was hindering my ability to do my job. Personally, I felt like my bosses had found their reason to get what they wanted: me out of the door. I could only see this going one way. I was following in Mike's footsteps all right, but not in a way I'd expected.

The problem with any toxic relationship is you often blame yourself too much. I am a huge advocate for owning your fate and taking control of the situation, but I'd allowed my superiors to belittle me to the point where I continuously blamed myself. For a period of time, their tactics worked, then I became more reflective and got heavily invested in self-development books. By blaming myself, I thought I was experiencing a *Task-Oriented Realization*—basically believing I didn't have the ability to work in education.

What I realized was, despite all of this accumulating over the course of three years, I had allowed myself to relinquish control because I felt I had none. I realized I had to take ownership of this and bury the misconceptions of others with results in a different setting. To be able to see your role in a situation and control the controllable factors is crucial to overcoming difficult times. Having been so close to leaving for the police force and the Royal Air Force, I decided to remain in education because I strongly believed I had something to offer. It was my *Purpose* to inspire, my calling to educate, and my destiny to help others.

I took my chance and applied to a new school. Changing the environment was something I could control, and the *Self-Realization* I had empowered me to grow in my independence. When you make a big call, expect big repercussions—for better or for worse.

Once I told my superiors of my intentions to leave for new pastures, the situation became increasingly turbulent. The difference this time is I had liberated myself from the emotional shackles the environment had placed on me. I was free to see out my remaining time there without worry. I had never seen my superiors more frustrated by the feedback I received from my future employer about how positive I was, how I would fit in at my new place of work, and how successful I could be as a teacher.

The lesson from this: I started to own the situation and understand other people may have flaws, the environment may be toxic, and the situation may not be ideal at home, but this does not mean you pander and allow your energy to be consumed by these negative sponges around you. It is ultimately up to you to assess for yourself and then change your behavior, change the people who surround you, change the environment, change the situation, or all of the above.

CHAPTER 5

Looking in the Mirror

In each of these timelines highlighted in my stories, an obstacle became apparent within my *Aspirations*, resulting in me realizing I didn't actually want the things I was aspiring to have. To face these obstacles, one must go through the *Realization* stage. To access this, becoming increasingly *reflective* is key. In every journey through personal development, there are always obstacles to overcome before reaching your goals.

There are four forms of *Realization*, but there is *one* truly effective pathway to take for all of these forms: taking ownership of the situation yourself.

The four types are:

1. *Situational Realization*
2. *Task-Oriented Realization*
3. *Realization of Others*
4. *Self-Realization*

SITUATIONAL

A first potential barrier to your *Purpose Cycle* could possibly be the situation you are in, such as a financial situation or a family situation. There are many barriers I have witnessed from friends or family:

"I was about to leave my job to pursue my dream, but then we had a child."

"I don't have enough money to start a business, and I can't get a bank loan to fund my start-up."

"The timing is just not right at this moment. Maybe next year."

Essentially, a *Situational Realization* is facing an obstacle that involves the environment around you and the external barriers between you and your goal. Sometimes the environment isn't right. Sometimes, the timing is not quite right. While I can appreciate your life changes when you have a family or take on a mortgage, there's nothing stopping you from implementing tiny changes in your life.

In the world we live in now, technology empowers people to pursue any *Aspiration* they have. For example: in your pocket you have the most incredible tool enabling you to start-up any store, website, content platform, or podcast you desire. It's called a phone! While you don't want to spend your life staring at a screen, there is always time (even thirty minutes per day) where you can work on your business. Just think about the hours you spend scrolling through Instagram or watching reality TV when you could be networking or building content.

Most *Situational Realizations* can be navigated. There are some pretty hard-hitting moments in life where postponing a dream is the only option, but that isn't to say the *Aspiration* dies there and then.

Some *Purpose Cycles* last decades, or longer. Don't completely ditch your dreams just because the timing isn't right. Prepare your dreams for when the timing does become right.

TASK-ORIENTED

A *Task-Oriented Realization* is confronting an obstacle that presents itself when trying to execute a task. When you aspire to be a multi-million-dollar business owner, the task at hand is simple, right? Build a multi-million-dollar business. This isn't always as simple as it appears in our dreams, and big goals often take many small actions to achieve. Any time a task appears achievable but then appears as a mountain to overcome, one is experiencing the *Realization* the task may not be as simple as one first thought.

A *Task-Oriented Realization* is often associated with those late-night worries: "Oh crap! What on earth have I gotten myself into?" kind of moments. Sound familiar? A lot of people have this type of *Realization* when they have done one of two things: made an overly ambitious promise, or actually began executing their plan.

It's the fear of the mountain that is yet to be climbed. This is where most people give up because it's just too damn difficult. I've once promised myself I was going to run forty kilometers a week for a month. Guess how long I kept my promise? I ran for two days, and on the morning of the third, I went to the gym instead to lift weights rather than run again. It masked my guilt temporarily because I diverted my goal to something that was still exercise, but guilt has its way of creeping up on you in the long-term. Very similar to people who promise to save more of their money. They may promise to save $200 a month but then withdraw $150 from their savings for a "special reason." They've still saved $50, but they've taken a shortcut on their goal.

Overly ambitious goals can often present themselves as a *Task-Oriented Realization*. I'm not telling you not to dream big, but having goals that seem too far away can demoralize you before you even get started. The key is to build areas in your life that will help you get to your goal.

Task-Oriented Realization can also work the other way and be somewhat uninspiring. For example, you may realize the career you wanted to climb so highly to the top of wasn't all what it was meant to be. I've seen this a lot with people coming into teaching. They see the TV adverts about the cups of tea in the staff room each day and the 3:30 p.m. finishes. The reality of teaching is quite the contrary, and some may realize the education sector may not be for them. This applies to other careers too, such as the police and emergency services. I'm sure a lot of people reading this book have started a new job and hated it. Be very careful when understanding when to go back to the *Aspiration* stage, though, because there are times when you just have to get through the task at hand.

One instance of this was a job I had when I returned from spending nine months in the United States of America. My

Aspiration in the twenty-three story was to start a business, but I knew the task wasn't attainable straight away. As part of the *Task-Oriented Realization,* I understood I had to build my way to that point. I could have taken shortcuts and become "a business owner" in some form. After visualizing the kind of business owner I wanted to be, I knew I needed to build foundations before taking the leap. I got a part-time job to provide for my basic needs and then built up my business slowly on the side. We'll delve into this more in the *Creation* phase.

The other form of *Task-Oriented Realization* is based upon the factors of volume. How much are you taking on? Do you have time to take on certain tasks? I believe you can make time for anything, but not everything. Therefore, you have to be extremely selective over what projects or tasks you take on, potentially even saying "no," which may upset some people. If they know what path you're on and understand your reasoning, then they will accept you have to prioritize other things right now, but they can't relate to something they are not aware of. Be honest from the outset and make it clear to those around you your time is precious, and you always want to be 100 percent present and focused in every moment.

REALIZATION OF OTHERS

At the point of beginning your *Purpose Cycle*, you may have spoken to friends, family, or colleagues about the prospect of what it is you want to achieve. You may have noticed a reaction or change in those people in your inner circles. Were they happy for you? Did you notice a change in how they acted around you? The *Realization of Others* is noticing the circle of people around you and how they influence your decisions and mindset. This can be in a positive way or a negative way.

In a negative context, this form of *Realization* makes you notice jealousy in others, a change in character, or even some of your most trusted inner circle residents attempting to pull you down with negative comments. You see this in companies where the young, ambitious trainee wants to climb to the top of head office while their older colleagues watch in disgust, talk negatively about them behind their back, and even start acting cold toward them. Some examples of this are shown in the TV show *Suits*. You quickly find out if a person's intentions are right for you when you are completely open and honest with them about your goals and visions for the future.

Rex Hudler, former baseball player, said in his 2008's essay, "Be a fountain, not a drain." A fountain would be somebody who adds value to other people's lives. They provide kindness, support, and care without expecting anything in return. Quite simply, you feel better after spending time with these types of people. The contrast: a drain. Drains take energy, and you feel empty after spending time with them. It is a classic comparison of optimist versus pessimist, positive mindset versus negative mindset, selfless versus selfish. Ensure you surround yourself with fountains while phasing out the drains from your inner circle. In addition to this, be the fountain you want to attract to yourself.

If you don't know any drains, then there are two possibilities: you either have a well-constructed positive circle, or you might not be able to identify the drains in your life yet. Most toxic behavior occurs in a subtle manner, and it is usually masked by the recipient due to their predetermined bias toward a person. Common mindsets are "my friend would never do that" or "my partner only wants what is best for me." It is important to identify drain-like behaviors from people so those who are in your circle of influence can have a positive effect on you rather than a negative one.

It might be that you've adopted a negative mindset and acted like a drain in the past. If that's the case, the next form of *Realization* is definitely for you.

SELF-REALIZATION

This is the most difficult but most effective form of *Realization*. The *Realization* that, actually, you might not (yet!) have the character, the skills, or the dedication to complete your *Purpose Cycle* due to unconfronted flaws you have not worked on. They may have been neglected or dismissed consciously only to appear later down the line, or you could have been completely oblivious to them until now. Do you really want to get out of your nice warm bed at 5:00 a.m. to chase greatness? Another reason the majority of people abandon their dreams at this stage is they realize they don't have what it takes to achieve their goal—but not due to a lack of talent.

It's due to a lack of self-esteem.

Karen Guthrie states in a 2021 article for the University of Illinois, "[If you have low self-esteem] it may be difficult for you to attain the goals you have set, resulting in an increased sense of failure. You may have a constant feeling that nothing that you do is right." A pathway to your goals is already going to be difficult without limiting beliefs, and as we worked on in the previous chapter, positive self-talk will lead to higher self-esteem. Guthrie explains, "Positive or high self-esteem helps us accomplish our goals and assists us in coping with life's challenges. If you have positive self-esteem, you have confidence in your abilities; you are not afraid to try new things."

It's true if a journey to success is easy, then everyone would do it. So, what makes *you* the person to do it?

There are two directions you can take at this stage. On the one hand, you could air out the good, the bad, and the ugly about yourself and face up to the flaws you have that you need to work on. On the other hand, you could carry on blaming other people and trying to control everything around you. I have had to face this difficult crossroads, and believe me, this was not a nice experience. It was like taking off a band-aid. You have to just accept there are aspects of yourself that aren't perfect and ask yourself what you can do better. To this day, I'm still working on my flaws, as everybody should. Ever since my late twenties, I realized the grief of my early twenties consumed me and exaggerated a number of already deep-lying flaws I possessed.

On *The High Performance Podcast*, there is a term Sir Chris Hoy, Olympic and world cycling champion, used called "the Father Christmas effect." This is when someone believes they never fail, they don't have any flaws, and everything they do is successful. They often state, "I never lose," and post only the positives on social media. Anyone you know spring to mind? If you are close with one of these types of people, you may have seen firsthand their world comes crashing down when they do fail (Humphrey, 2021). This is because they have given themselves no contingency for bumps in the road or obstacles to overcome. Once they lose, their dream is over. This is why it is crucial you set your mindset *before* embarking on this journey. It is also why there are two steps in the *Purpose Cycle* before you actually begin working on your goals.

You need to promote an environment where your closest friends, spouse, and family members can be open with you and tell you what they feel your areas of personal development should be, maybe a toxic trait that you have, or how you can communicate better with those closest to you.

Once you have been through this experience, you have maneuvered the greatest obstacle: yourself. If you haven't managed to do this, then it could be that your *Purpose Cycle* begins again with a new *Aspiration* because the current one isn't meant for you. This process isn't designed for you to gain the opportunity that isn't right for you. This process is designed for you to gain the opportunity that *is* right for you!

HOW TO NAVIGATE *REALIZATION*
All of these forms of *Realization* can be categorized under one umbrella term:

Excuses.

Yes, there may be tangible obstacles standing in your way or peers who shower negativity on you. There may be a lack of knowing where to even begin your journey, and there may be a child relying on your regular, stable income to feed them. As long as you see them as obstacles, these excuses will quickly personify into drains when they could work in your favor as fountains. Understand the analogy of drains and fountains apply to jobs, opportunities, and situations as well as are personified in people. Everything in the universe has a vibration that exudes a positive or negative connotation.

Blame culture is rife among the current generation. It always seems to be somebody else's fault, or the world was against them, or even, "I just can't seem to get a lucky break." It is evident in our society, and I'm sure we've either been guilty of this ourselves, or we know somebody who has a victim mindset. I could write down a million and one excuses I have heard in my over thirty years on this planet, and I could even add a few more I have made myself. The point is, do these excuses ever move you forward? If you have any of those challenges I mentioned, such as kids, unstable income, or doubters in your inner circle, you have the greatest advantage of all—fuel.

BATTLING CRIPPLING INSECURITY.

Beating your *Self-Realization* can be tricky, especially when you suffer from insecurities already. You need to source where these insecurities originated from. Quite often, people confuse insecurity with something they have done to themselves to cause it. What you will find when you dig deep is insecurity is often triggered by others and, more surprisingly, particularly those closest to you. This is because, above all, you value the opinions of those closest to you the most, so a passing comment, a backhanded compliment, or a strong disliking of something you do can have a long-standing effect if you are a person who does not value yourself as highly as you should.

Of course, the opinions of those closest to you are important. After all, we are innately programmed to seek approval from others. It's in our nature to want to feel belonging within a group, feel loved by a partner, or have others feel proud of what you are doing (Larsen, 1976). Without a shadow of a doubt, I have learned there is no opinion more important than the one you hold for yourself. The opinion must be informed of experiences *you* have gone through, not somebody else. Raymond Nickerson in *Review of General Psychology* 2 defines confirmation bias as "the term is typically used in the psychological literature, connotes the seeking or interpreting of evidence in ways that are partial to existing beliefs, expectations, or a hypothesis in hand."

A person who comments on your outfit is doing so based on the premise of their own fashion taste. A person who comments on your career *Aspirations* is doing so based on their own understanding of success and whether they think negatively of people for having more or less of it.

People may tailor their opinions of what you should be doing to suit their own narrative, but we could also fall into the trap of our own confirmation bias. This is why it is important to take an objective view of yourself and not allow any limiting beliefs to dictate your journey. Just like you wouldn't allow a negative person to become a drain for your goals, don't become your own drain.

Ultimately, battling insecurity is all about you becoming comfortable with the complete you—who in fact is the only person who knows the complete you. You frame a version of yourself for your partner, for your parents, or for your friends. It is only over time spent consistently with a person in an intimate setting you gradually see the layers to that complete person. From flaws, traits, characteristics, positives, and ego, you know yourself better than anybody—so it's only right you hold the overall judgment on yourself.

One other form of insecurity is when the individual assumes if they begin their journey, the world will come crashing down, and the worst possible scenario they could think of will become true. This is called "catastrophizing." To avoid this, just simply think to yourself, "How many times have I assumed the worst, and it has actually happened?"

I have been a victim of this many times and thought, "My YouTube video is going to get one view, and everyone will ridicule me," or, "I will embarrass myself on radio, and everyone will know I'm a nervous wreck." I've even thought, "This staff training session will go terribly, and I will be outed as a fraud!"

USE YOUR MINDSET TO TURN NEGATIVE ENERGY INTO POSITIVE ENERGY

Did any of these things ever happen to me? No, the worst thing that happened was a few people laughed at me making

YouTube videos! Did that stop me? No! The best thing about it was I just nodded and laughed along, deep in the knowledge I was using their laughter as fuel to continue. If people are talking about your ambitions behind your back, then that shows more about their own mindset than yours. I decided to reframe how I viewed their opinions by turning them into fountains. I welcomed their words and grew the content I made. In turn, you'll start to notice these comments fade away as you prove negative comments don't deter you.

Doubters and critics are needed in life because, as human beings, we can't please everyone, nor should we try to, but it is dangerous to only listen to people who tell you what you want to hear. Using the words of others to drive you on is taking a negative situation and turning it into a positive outcome. Be careful not to stray too far on this path and only work out of spite. The funniest thing about this situation for me was, once I stopped and moved on to a different project, the very same people said, "Jon, why aren't you making videos anymore? I actually enjoyed them." It just goes to show these people are actually invested in what you're doing with your life, so utilize this to drive you forward.

See, it never turns out as catastrophic as you envision prior to starting.

The key characteristic for the *Realization* phase is having a reflective personality. When you go through the *Realization* process, the viewpoint is always in the form of hindsight. Being reflective, however, isn't just looking back on a situation and thinking about what could have been different. It is about digging deep into what was in your control and taking responsibility for events that have gone by. Once you take ownership and reflect accordingly, you begin to grow.

STARTING AGAIN

Many people go through the *Realization* phase and give up. They discover barriers and choose to remain safe. Don't get this confused with starting again. This is taking a step back because you know it will result in taking two steps forward.

To start again means you have analyzed a situation, broken it down to a point where you can make a decision informed by research and insight, and then listened to your gut instinct.

Take Mark Zuckerberg, for example: on the fourth of February 2004, Zuckerberg launched Facebook from his Harvard dorm room. His *Aspiration* came from the fact he came across an idea in his prep school of a student directory. This was called "The Photo Address Book," which students referred to as "The Facebook." Such photo directories were an important part of the student social experience at many private schools. With them, students were able to list attributes such as their class years, their friends, and their telephone numbers (Kirkpatrick, 2011).

Zuckerberg's Facebook then became an internal pursuit, and he initially kept it within Harvard. Upon having what I refer to as the *Task-Oriented Realization*, he realized he would need help expanding this project and enlisted roommate Dustin Moskovitz to assist his vision. They began with Columbia University, New York University, Stanford,

Dartmouth, Cornell, University of Pennsylvania, Brown, and Yale (Kirkpatrick, 2011).

Following the success of the early stages of Facebook, Zuckerberg had a second *Realization* in which he learned to fulfill this *Purpose Cycle* (Facebook), he must start again elsewhere. What was initially an *Aspiration* to get to know his classmates and help others do the same ended up being an *Aspiration* to build a complete social network. Moskovitz and some friends moved to Palo Alto, California, in Silicon Valley, where they leased a small house that served as an office. Over the summer, Zuckerberg met Peter Thiel, who invested in the company. They got their first office in mid-2004, and the rest, they say, is history (Kirkpatrick, 2011).

Now before you pick up the laptop to type your "I quit!" email, I'm not telling everyone to drop out of university, quit their jobs, and leave town for the pursuit of their dreams. What I am giving here is an example of somebody who understood the risk he was taking but believed in an idea so much he was willing to put everything into his idea with conviction and a relentless drive that got him to where he is today. It could be that to progress to be a CEO of a company, you have to move to a smaller start-up and build it up yourself. It could even be to find true happiness in a relationship, you have to suffer the short-term pain of being single rather than the constant long-term pain of being unhappy in a relationship that isn't right for you.

RESISTANCE TO GROWTH

As you categorize your *Realizations*, you will begin to make positive changes. However, one of the big changes you will notice in the *Realization* stage is the change in others. By this point, you're psyched about beginning a new chapter in your life. You are bursting with motivation and ready to set the alarm clock and seize the day! The feeling of anticipation *should* excite you. After all, many people do fall in love with the process, especially when they know the process is going to take them places. Be careful not to assume everyone is going to be stoked for you.

There will be occurrences when *Realization of Others* takes place, and you know who your true friends are. Some people act as parasites of success and will try to live off your victories, but did you see them while you were climbing the mountain? Having an extremely solid idea of who truly belongs in your inner circle is important before you set off on your journey to success. Know your value; only allow people to be a part of your life if they can stick with you through the rough times as well as the happy times.

The most difficult task of all is shrinking your inner circle. The vast majority of us do this as we progress through our twenties and thirties anyway because, well, who wants two hundred friends when you're thirty? It's exhausting to maintain a few close relationships at times, especially if you're an introvert like me. What really gives me energy is being selective with the people I spend my time with. This way, I know I have a high-value *quality* of relationships rather than a low-value *quantity*.

In *Jim Rohn's 8 Best Success Lessons* by Chris Widener, Rohn states, "You're the average of the five closest people to you." Ultimately, you are in control of your own identity, but the more fountains you surround yourself with, the more you will grow into the person you want to become. Think about who you're closest to and what characteristics they have that inspire you to be a better person. In addition to this, what characteristics do *you* have that make you a great person to be around? When embarking on this journey, it is important to be continuously reflective and aware you cannot just blame everyone else for what has previously happened or the situation you are currently in. As I mentioned previously, some people (do what drains do), and it's important to remove them from your life where possible. That said, if you constantly blame others for your failings, you'll soon be facing the ugly truth alone: the fact that you're the problem. Then you realize who the true problem was, and that is an ugly truth—believe me.

You may have a few people in mind who seem to just drag you down. They sap energy from you in each minute you spend with them. You could buy them a bouquet of flowers, and they would tell you they prefer another type of flower. You could tell them about this exciting project you're working on, and they'll cut you off to change the subject to about them. What's important is to slowly phase these people out. You may not even have to cut them out of your lives completely because better the devil you know, right? What *is* important is they are not welcome in your inner circle of influence because that is where they can do the damage that will ultimately lead to sabotaging your entire *Purpose Cycle*.

Many people are too afraid of making that big call of cutting off somebody, starting again on their own, or "taking a backward step" in their work because of the immediate struggle or pain they will endure. Think back to the previous chapter: Who do you actually want to become? Always vote for your future, ideal self, even if it means a short-term spell of struggle. You'll come out the other end better for it. No matter how daunting the step appears, always understand it is a step closer to the person you want to become.

CHAPTER 6

Tasks

———

TASK 4—UNDERSTANDING YOUR INNER CIRCLE

For your next task, you are going to take a look at your *inner circle*. Who would you define as the five to ten people to whom you are the closest? Who do you immediately think to tell when you have good news? Who do you seek advice from? Now visualize them during your success. To do this, I want you to think of the end goal—*Fruition*. What does *Fruition* look like when you achieve it? What about the adversity and *Realizations* you overcame in your vision? Did you see any of your inner circle helping you on your way there?

Take a piece of paper and a pen and picture in your head the vision of you gathering your inner circle into a room and announcing your intentions to achieve *Fruition*.

Picture the reactions of each member of your inner circle:

- How did they react?
- What did they say to you?

- Which members of your inner circle dismissed your news and then announced their unrelated "big news" too? (Be aware that friends who show empathy by comparing their experiences aren't raining on your parade, they are relating to your situation).

Write down three negative comments your inner circle said to you in your vision:

1.
2.
3.

Now, it is really important you look at these comments and think, "Is this what they are saying, or is this what *I am saying about myself*?"

The reason for this is that you may potentially be catastrophizing. Do you feel like those closest to you actually hold you in such low esteem? I don't know the people you trust most, but I highly doubt this is the case.

Now, write down three positive comments your inner circle said to you in your vision:

1.
2.
3.

The next step: you actually tell your inner circle your *Aspirations*. This is a really positive step for two reasons:

1. You understand a situation in your head planned out in the worst possible case never actually turns out that way.
2. Congratulations, you are now accountable for your actions because you've just publicly announced your plans. How do you feel? Scared? Good! Excited? Even better! The best part of this task is your plans are becoming a reality. You've begun speaking it into existence.

In the previous chapter, we looked at your self-talk. You worked on reframing yourself as a positive person. In this next task, we will work on reframing situations to work to your advantage, reframing haters into fuel, and reframing failures into learning opportunities.

TASK 5—REFRAMING OPPORTUNITIES OF REALIZATION

For this next task, you need to split a blank page down the middle into two columns.

On the left-hand side, you are going to write down a challenge you've faced. It could be at any time during your life, or it could be the day-to-day challenges you overcome. It could even be the many forms of *Realization* you encounter (*Situational, Task-Orientated, Realization of Others*, and *Self-Realization*).

On the right-hand side, you are going to write down the lessons you learned or can learn from each of these challenges. Think about your friends when they ask you for advice. Do you always tell them you agree with their catastrophizing, or do you tell them to think optimistically? You always tell them to look on the bright side, "It will turn out okay," as you put your arm around them. Why not do that for yourself? This is an interesting concept called "holding space." Connor Beaton defines "holding space" as. "the process of witnessing and validating someone else's emotional state while simultaneously being present to your own."

We often provide our peers with the perfect holding space to assist when they have an issue. This is why we become their go-to person when a crisis emerges. However, what about providing ourselves with our own holding space? This links to the self-love tasks in the *Aspiration* section.

When each of these challenges passes, look at the piece of paper to reflect on the challenges. Did the situation turn out as bad as you first thought? Of course, they didn't! Did you build on the lessons you wrote down? If you didn't, then what lessons did you learn? Remember: every challenge comes with a lesson. Always make sure that you fail forward.

Good job! You are now beginning to reframe situations to suit you.

LESSONS LEARNED FROM *REALIZATION*

1. *Task-Oriented Realization* and *Realization of Others* **are tough because you have to take control of a situation that seems beyond your control.** Reframing this with a mindset that frees you from the shackles of "blame culture" is uplifting.
2. **Realizing the task is more difficult than imagined may put you off—but if it were easy to be successful, then everyone would be living a successful life.** The question

is, are you willing to put that amount of consistent effort over time?

3. **You can view the world from any lens you choose.** When you realize nobody else really cares about the small habits you acquire each day, you will feel liberated and grateful that the only person who is responsible for your own journey is you.

Three lessons I've learned about myself from **Realization** *is:*

1.
2.
3.

Key Character trait: **Reflectiveness**

PART 3

INITIATION

CHAPTER 7

Taking Risks

———

21

Freedom. Stepping off the plane back in the UK was liberating: the unshackling from the rest of the group had been granted by Anthony. Although he showed wisdom by suggesting we fly home rather than get the coach back, he had no real idea of the struggles tormenting my day-to-day routine.

Following my *Situational Realization*, I understood I had to tackle this battle myself. It was only a matter of days until I was set to hand in my dissertation—less than forty-eight hours. Following that, I was set to embark on a trip to North Carolina in the United States of America to coach "soccer" for nine months. After a *Realization,* a person faces a crossroads: restart a new cycle with a new *Aspiration* or continue on with your journey. For me, a new *Aspiration* was born: to be that "key figure" in an organization and feel a sense of belonging. This was probably somewhat related to my younger self's ambitions of being accepted. I had yet to discover searching for belonging is a dangerous path. Belonging was so ambiguous to me I couldn't define it any more than a hamster on a wheel can define its destination. The pot of gold is always further away. Tangible goals were a kind of *Self-Realization* made in hindsight, which I was set to discover on my trip.

With all journeys, the most important step of the journey is the next one.

Two eye-blinking days later, I was unshackled from uni, and upon my *Realization of Others*, I was aware I didn't want to be like those figures I'd admired as a fresh-faced eighteen-year-old. I almost felt guilty their wealth of authority, power, and fulfillment was centered around a social group in university. I initially carried a huge amount of guilt for how I let myself down. It wasn't the fact I wanted to be a part of the group because there were some fantastic people in that group. I had let myself down by acting a certain way just to feel accepted in this group. Taking responsibility is important. Just like alcohol is not always a bad thing, it can sometimes make you act completely out of line with your values. Social groups, people, jobs, and stressful environments can make you do the same. It might not be toxic for everybody, but if it is toxic for you, then you must take note and adapt.

The feeling of guilt is perfectly normal when you awaken to the fact you've not been acting in alignment with your true self. The stages of the *Purpose Cycle* often overlap because *Realization* can occur during any step. It can often send you back a step to revisit your *Aspirations* and aim for something different and greater. It can also happen while you are entering a new phase. I was taking the first steps toward my true self, and I was excited to discover more about myself. My priorities had changed after my epiphany during the trip to Spain. I now aspired to be a sports coach who eventually owned his own sports coaching company. America was the first step in the process of redesigning the new me. This step is called *Initiation.*

My parents had shown some resistance to the idea of me traveling to America. My mother did not want me to "get into trouble," while my father would have much preferred it if I had gotten a job and joined the "real" working world. I, of course, had other plans—much bigger plans—and it all commenced as I boarded the flight at Manchester Airport. It was a risky move, considering I knew nobody out there. All I had to go on was a Skype interview with the company I had chosen, but it was a risk I had to take. This move would turn out to be my start—something that eventually would propel me to levels above where I thought I could be.

Initiation is all about taking the first steps into the unknown. I referred to choosing your level of discomfort earlier, and I consciously decided to make choices that would plunge me into the unknown, but what I knew would benefit me. In a slightly different context, I relate it to the scene in *Good Will Hunting* by Van Sant, where Matt Damon's character is referring to his childhood. His abusive stepfather used to ask him to choose between an instrument to be beaten with, a wrench, a stick, or a belt. Robin Williams's character says, "I've got to go with the belt," to which Matt Damon replies, "I used to go with the wrench." When asked why, he says, "Because f**k him, that's why." This attitude toward life of opting for the tough road to make you stronger is what shapes a person to develop a bulletproof mindset. I knew moving to the states would be uncomfortable, withdrawing myself from that social circle would be unpopular, and adopting a new culture, life, and job would be terrifying. I wanted to start choosing the wrench in life.

Ten swift hours passed, and I touched down on American soil: Charlotte, North Carolina. I soaked up every moment, "Welcome to the United States of America."

Wow.

As I stepped on the escalator to retrieve my luggage, I gazed up at this enormous sea of stars and stripes as the largest flag I had ever seen was placed in clear sight for the arrivals to marvel at. The national flag draped across the wall facing the escalator. The US national anthem played in my head. Every single frame of this movie-like experience was unfolding in front of me. What an incredible feeling it was. I paid myself the credit I deserved for allowing my inner *Aspiration* to take its course. I thought back to being on that coach heading to Salou when I could never articulate what it was I wanted. I only knew what I didn't want.

This is what I wanted.

I very quickly landed back down to Earth. Ben, my new boss, was awaiting my arrival with a pair of car keys in his hand. "Hey Jon, hope you had a good trip! Let's head to your first venue."

My first three days would be spent in a hotel prior to meeting my very first host family. Ben handed me the keys, and I was confused.

"Here's your ride."

Parked in front of me was a 2012 Chevrolet Cruz. My first task was to drive two-and-a-half hours to a city called Fayetteville. I was terrified, but as I thought back to the last ride I'd taken in a foreign country with the football team, suddenly this one didn't seem so bad.

I fell at the first hurdle. "Jon! That's the wrong side. Welcome to the USA, buddy!"

The second test, I failed just as badly. I turned on the ignition and began to rock backward and forward profusely. I couldn't work out what was going on. I had no GPS, and all I could witness was my new boss driving out of the parking lot while my car looked like it was doing the Cha Slide!

Choose the wrench, Jon.

He turned his car around. "Jon, you can't use both feet for driving! Use the right foot only! Welcome to the USA, brother!"

How many times will I hear that?

My *Realization* at this moment was that I was a terrible driver of automatic cars—probably because I'd never sat in one before. My other *Realization* was in the first forty minutes of being in this country, I had learned so much.

This was going to be a great trip! I'd reframed a disaster into a massive learning opportunity, and off I drove to my first destination with my adrenaline flowing, heart rate through the roof, and my thoughts still thirty-six thousand feet in the air! I had a few hours to process these feelings. What I came to learn is that driving is a great way to think deeply and reflect. I felt strangely comfortable in discomfort. This was the birth of a new me, one who loved challenges and was curious about what the next day brought. This was my first clear recollection of the *Initiation* phase—a reinvention of who I was beforehand. Many people feel the same when they move to new towns or to a new country. That "fresh start" feeling is a springboard for opportunity. For the rest of the journey, I visualized all I wanted to become and what I sought from this whole experience.

25

Now another eighteen months wiser as a business holder, I had begun laying the foundations for my exit plan from the coaching business I had started at the tender age of twenty-three. Over the months that had passed, I felt like I had put my ambitions on standby as I embarked on my route to becoming a primary school teacher.

The beauty of owning my own business was it was me who went into the schools to pitch for business and then delivered the sessions to the schools that hired me. This led to multiple schools becoming interested in either taking me on full-time or, in one school's case, in particular, wanting to pay for me to enroll in a teacher training program. The latter offer I gratefully accepted and prepared myself to part company with the business. The business was once an *Aspiration* but now did nothing but cost me a huge amount of self-confidence and paid me little more than a pittance. I mentioned in the previous section that self-confidence affects your ability to succeed. Having multiple school leaders show belief in me gave me the self-confidence I lacked for over eighteen months. I was back again.

Initiation is all about making that first step. As you saw in the previous section from my twenty-one timeline, I *had* to board that plane to begin pursuing my goal of becoming a coach. In this timeline, I *had* to take responsibility for my own decisions and remove myself from an environment that would not have gotten me anywhere. I *had* to choose the wrench. Don't get me wrong, at that point in time, the business was turning over profit and was never once in debt. I'd managed to run it successfully as a solo mission. However, there was no room for growth, expansion, or long-term route to becoming the leading organization for sports coaching in the region. It was very safe in the short-term but dangerously unambitious in the long-term. I was almost treading that fine line of a dead-end job. My thoughts were if you're going to do something, you may as well try and be the best.

If I was stifled in this particular field, then I had to go back to *Aspiration* and revise my long-term ambitions. I decided teaching was a route I wanted to go down. I had the *Situational Realization* that my current environment was not right for me. I also looked at myself and realized I had flaws that needed addressing. Once I felt ready to take myself to the next step on the *Purpose Cycle*, I began to *Initiate* my actions toward becoming a teacher.

I had an extremely uncomfortable yet weight-relieving meeting with the co-owner Dan in which we agreed to close the business and share the remaining profit 50/50. I decided to use my share to invest in myself and pay for my teaching training. Investing in myself was a habit I wanted to start. This was a far cry from my university self—a person who could not focus and struggled with the education system due to my own maturity levels as a learner.

My previous *Purpose Cycle*, which took me from the pits of a university trip to Salou across the Atlantic, taught me how to grow into a self-reflective, independent learner. I knew my journey in learning was only just beginning. I began to consciously invest in myself. Rather than wasting money on nights out drinking, possessions I didn't need, and paying no attention to my bank balance, I started to be aware of how I could improve my opportunities by enrolling in courses and spending money on my health. *Initiation* is the most exciting of the steps because you see the path of what you could become lighting up in front of you.

Fast forward to my first day away from the business. Upon entering the school gates for the first time, the future of my career lit up in front of me just like I had envisioned. This *Purpose Cycle* meant more than any of those that preceded it, and I felt like this was a point in my life, at twenty-five years old, that this step was the greatest of all. This time around, I was correct. Making a positive change is never guaranteed. A move considered to be bold or brave must be calculated, but there will always be an element of risk. We never truly know how a life decision will turn out. However, I've always been optimistic enough to be grateful for every turn I've made, as it has ultimately led me to where I am now. The fear hit again, which can often strike during the scary yet exciting *Initiation* phase. As long as you acknowledge the emotion, process it, and feel it without letting it become part of your identity, then the limiting beliefs won't creep back.

28

I had to change my environment, but many people thought the move was too much of a risk.

"You don't know how good you've got it here," mentioned a senior colleague.

There were similar doubts from other colleagues; a few teachers had sought greener pastures before and came to regret that decision. I got the sense they thought something similar was happening with me. *Initiation* can send people one of two ways: you revert back to comfort, or you take the leap of faith. I chose to take that leap away from my toxic safety net. I had already begun initiating the next step in my cycle. In my new workplace, I felt comfortable, trusted, and valued, but this also comes at an exciting and valuable price.

A quote from one of my childhood films, *Spider-Man*, springs to mind when Peter Parker's uncle says, "With great power, comes great responsibility" (Ziskin et al. 2002). It could also be added that with great trust comes great responsibility. In his book *Greenlights,* Matthew McConaughey talks about "Chasing your hero." He was asked, "Who's your hero?" and he said, "Me, in ten years." The premise of this is his hero is always the version of himself that is ten years away. He's never going to beat his hero, but he can always aspire to be his best self. That is what *Initiation* is about. I was setting out to be my hero in ten years. Yes, Mike was a big influence on the type of leader I wanted to become, but I had to be my own version. I had to chase my own hero.

I had never thought of a role model like this before, only a person who had already achieved what I wanted to accomplish in the *Fruition* stage. This is where your *Aspiration* turns internal and becomes an inspiration.

During the first phase, you saw how your *Fruition* looked to somebody else. *Initiation* is about seeing how your *Fruition* looks in your own frame. A new colleague called this workplace a "Forever school," but there was something distinctly true about her statement which inspired me. This could be the place in which I grow and become all I am determined to be. Maybe this was the place to be the "hero" I had aspired to be a little over two years ago. I could see the route mapped out to me now, clearer than ever. To be somebody else's Mike was an inspiring thought.

Simon Sinek in *Leaders Eat Last* tells you to "Be the leader that you wish you had." My precedent was set early on, and I feel like I can bring qualities to my colleagues that I wished I had in previous years. The greatest feeling hit me when I entered this new establishment: everyone was being a leader. Rank doesn't dictate true leaders, people do. What I was surrounded by was a culture I couldn't have even dreamed of orchestrating myself. This was all brought together by someone who I would consider to be a new mentor to myself. His trust in me became apparent in the very opening days of working at my new haven.

"Jon, I need you to lead a whole school staff meeting on these," he confidently instructed while handing me a Chromebook.

I took a look at one of these alien devices, gulped, and then went home to begin my research on how I could turn myself into an expert. These were newly purchased for the school to use, and I could now admit (between us) I had never seen one of these devices in my life. I was trusted to lead, educate, and implement a brand-new strategy to an already established team of people I had not met before. It was an exhilarating feeling. The hit felt addictive; this was a taste of the *Fruition*, and I was prepared to pursue it even further. I gained a huge boost of self-confidence because, for the first time, I didn't need to seek gratification externally because internally, I felt empowered. Brilliant leaders do that for you.

A really important part of tasting the small part of *Fruition* that could come later down the line is you are not satisfied with that dopamine hit. You want to use those positive emotions to pursue it in the flesh. Once you have the first experience of success, you will start to delve into the unknown more and more. You begin to train yourself for future *Purpose Cycles* before you are ready.

Although I felt empowered, I wasn't yet established within my new team. Therefore, I had to continue to align with the parameters that would make me a successful version of myself. The initial feeling is a great start, and we sometimes get this when purchasing a new gym membership or test-driving a new car. It temporarily puts you in the shoes of events that could potentially come to *Fruition*. Use this as confirmation this is the path you are going to pursue and a reason *not* to kick back to *Aspiration* this time.

Each of these steps felt like huge risks. Growth occurs in its greatest form outside of the comfort zone, and you may feel the fear of failure. However, taking risks is a huge part of the *Initiation* phase. They feel like huge steps because it is *you* who has to take them, which is why it is often easier to give advice to others but not follow your own. The crippling fear of the first step can do that to us, but let's be honest, if it was easy, everybody would do it. So, what makes *you* the person to do it?

The answer is simple. You have thought about this step for a while because you have *Aspired* to be the end product. You have also *Realized* the enormity of the task you want to accomplish and understand your strengths and flaws. In the next chapter, you will take active steps to rewire your habits. You are now actively taking strides to pursue success. The very fact you are reading this book shows your desire to succeed, which sets you apart from another version of you who could be sitting in a low-challenge life, with stale potential and a mundane routine—unaware of the potential you have. The great thing is you may have been oblivious to this way of living and thought you were happy as you were, but can you ever go back to that lifestyle? Think back to the Dunning-Kruger effect: The more you know, the more you realize what there is yet to discover (Kruger et al. 2003).

CHAPTER 8

Plant Your Bamboo

The Chinese bamboo tree is a fascinating plant. They can patiently lie deep underground for up to five years, securing their roots and laying the foundations for growth. Then one day, the sun will rise, and the bamboo tree can burst through the soil, shooting up to eighty feet in the air in just six weeks!

To the human eye, it appears instant and by chance, when it was a cumulative effort after five years of tenacious work behind-the-scenes where nobody could witness the *Initiation* of its *Purpose*. The easiest part of *Initiation* is starting when your peers are aware of what you are doing. Those are the first few days when friends and family are checking in and asking how the new venture is going and how their new gym buddy is doing in those first sessions. What happens when nobody is watching? Do you truly act with the same consistency and conviction?

At the end of the journey, those same peers will witness your results, but there is likely going to be a period of time between the two where nobody will witness the habitual effort you make each day. The Chinese bamboo tree does not depend on its growth on what day of the week it is, what the other trees think of its journey, or the limiting beliefs embedded during its childhood. Use this example to mirror your own growth. Plant your bamboo.

Initiation uses internal triggers to ensure you make that first step. It's easy to confuse *Initiation* with inspiration, but they aren't the same thing. In this context, *Initiation* means taking action. You can feel inspired but do nothing, just like you can feel anxious and do something. What is important is you actually take the leap of faith and begin. A popular quote attributed to Confucius says, "We all have two lives, and the second one begins when we realize that we only have one" (Tygielski, 2021). This is the most exciting step, the most terrifying step, the boldest step, and the most enthralling step on your journey. The first day of the rest of your life and the day the ink touches down on the blank canvas is a new chapter in your story.

The ficklest emotion you can experience is motivation. To be motivated feels like a mere shot of insulin to the average person. It is a temporary rush of feelings that can often spark a chain of unsustainable events: you throw out all of your junk food, you buy "8 Minute Abs" videos, you even decide to quit bad habits such as smoking or drinking. Most of these temporary fixes make you feel better because of the anticipation of the action, in addition to the fact the action can grant you approval from others. Take this example, for instance: joining the gym. Once you pay the sign-on fee for a gym, you get a rush of accomplishment from merely signing up. The act of joining a gym is more of a dopamine hit than the act of actually going to the gym. For many, that is a feeling of dread more than anything else. The first few sessions are easy before they skip the odd session due to being "tired from work," and then they fall back into old habits.

That is the key: *habits.*

Your habits determine your overall identity, and your overall identity determines how you perceive yourself. James Clear, the author of *Atomic Habits*, discusses the concept of habit loops. Developing positive habit loops in the *Initiation* phase is crucial to setting yourself up for success.

First of all, Clear talks about the cue: "the cue triggers your brain to initiate a behavior. It is a bit of information that predicts a reward." Prehistorically, these would be our survival instincts for food, to go hunting, procreate, or find a mate. Nowadays, the cues are closely attributed to luxuries and success (money, fame, social status). The cues naturally lead to a craving, which is the brain's association with a cue.

When cravings occur, the brain links with the reward associated with the habit, not the habit itself. The brain speculates the craving is greater than what the feeling actually is. For example, gambling addicts develop the craving triggered by the cue of the sound played in casinos of coins hitting the tray. Naturally, we will gravitate to the easiest response with the least amount of friction when cravings occur. If we find comfort in lighting a cigarette or ordering fast food, then the response will follow the craving with ease. The friction caused by saying "no," or cooking a healthy meal is the right choice, but not the one a person makes due to the difficulty of breaking a habit.

Clear talks about the rewards associated with habits: "We chase rewards because they serve two purposes: (1) they satisfy us and (2) they teach us."

The reward is there to answer the craving. If a reward teaches us a negative message, it could persuade us not to pursue that particular craving again. E.g., those who have a bad experience with a particular type of food may stay away from it in the future. If any of those four parts don't work in unison, then a habit won't form. It is important to understand the process of forming a habit so you can: A) form positive habits, and B) identify times when you are forming a negative one.

When I think of cues, I try to ensure these are obvious to my conscious mind. This could include placing your gym mat in the middle of the room, so you remind yourself to stretch each morning, setting an alarm to drink more water, or even changing the trigger of a negative habit loop that causes you to have a cigarette (e.g., drinking) so that instead you do something instead, like chew gum.

YOUR NEW HABITS WON'T FORM INSTANTLY, BUT YOUR NEW IDENTITY WILL

Many people flicker from *Realization* to *Aspiration* and then back and forth for a long, long time. This is because they expect instant gratification: They start a business, and they want instant profit. They go to the gym, and they expect to be in the best shape of their lives. What those people forget is results are compounded over time with a level of consistency that is required for the benefits of positive habits to become evident (a.k.a. *Fruition*). Think of it as interest accumulating in your savings accounts stored in your bank. The interest will accumulate over time. If you withdraw your money after year one, then what is the point? Be proud you are aligning with your new identity, an upgraded version of yourself. The habits will compile over time.

The *Initiation* stage is all about what you are going to do now. It's about taking action; it's about laying the foundations for the future. The layers you set now are going to have a huge impact on your life a decade from now. Just think about that for a second: what would your "hero"—a version of you who is ten years your senior—expect from you now? What do you have to do for that future you to have the *Fruition* (and possibly the long-term fulfillment) it desires? If you feel like you aren't moving forward, then why not? A Chinese proverb states, "The best time to plant a tree was twenty years ago, and the second-best time to plant a tree is now." So, let's plant a bamboo tree.

UNSHACKLING YOURSELF FROM YOUR *REALIZATIONS*

To move forward and build new habits, you must first completely relinquish past belief systems from your persona. Your past experiences can help shape you—but not define you.

The reason for this is it can lead us down a path of spite. Using negativity to initiate a new journey can provide a powerful jump-start toward your goals, but similar to motivation, these feelings are finite and can often provide a greater lull when success comes.

If you do have that "chip on your shoulder," then you will often find "proving Mr. Smith wrong" won't fill you with the *Fruition* you desire mainly because you are seeking external validation. Do you really believe your schoolteacher from thirty years ago who said you'll "never amount to anything" will care that you've gone through all of that hard work for them? You must choose your pathway to your goals to satisfy yourself and grant yourself the internal validation for the person you've become for *you*, not somebody else. The same goes for changing to prove an ex-partner wrong or a former boss. Those people are in the past for a reason, and they don't deserve to influence the future you.

With *Initiation* now in full flow, you can focus on the early stages of your journey and reward yourself for taking the brave steps many people talk about but never act on.

PROPS FOR PROGRESSION
Items associated with a task for you to begin or complete a task are what I like to call "props for progression." These can have both a positive and negative effect on building your new identity by associating your ambitions with the external trigger rather than deep within yourself.

A negative way to use props to make you feel like you're winning could be, for example: purchasing a ton of new active wear for your newly developed goal to go to the gym. It could also be buying clothes two sizes too small in the hope one day a fad diet will allow the person to fit in them. Even spending the majority of income on a Rolex to be accepted within a new social circle is a negative way to use props. The commonality of these props is they are what it says on the tin—props. In reality, these external factors will never give you the longevity you are seeking. There are short bursts of external validation that will soon burn out when you realize they don't align with your *Purpose*, and they don't give you the internal validation you're seeking.

On the other hand, small props for progression can be a positive change, such as buying a fruit bowl if you want to eat more fruit. The subconscious trigger of the fruit being in view would make a person much more likely to eat fruit and therefore replenish the fruit bowl while shopping.

It is a matter of knowing which props are beneficial to your growth and which ones are toxic (if you're rewarding your efforts to your fitness goals with a pizza, you're being counterproductive). The fact is props for progression can be useful so long as the person implementing the props has the actual intent to act on the moves they want to make. If you ask somebody else for their opinion on if buying the Rolex will give you acceptance within a new crowd, you would get varied answers, but there is a strong case for purchasing a fruit bowl to help you eat more fruit. Catch my drift? The props need to have a use that can be identified objectively, not subjectively.

As a way of internally driving progress, you need to use these props as a reward rather than a trigger. This shifts the focus from positive reinforcement (if you do this, you will get this reward) to negative punishment (removing a reward or privilege as a result of not performing the desired action). Because you are now acting in accordance with your *new identity*, you should remind yourself with the operant conditioning strategy of negative punishment (Department of Psychology and Brain Science at the IOWA University).

To summarize, props for progressions are not sustainable, although the idea of them is. It is important to reward yourself as a method of operant conditioning to cement certain habits into your identity. As you hold yourself accountable, you will reward yourself less and punish yourself more the more a new habit becomes an expected behavior. The negative punishment is vital if you don't follow through with your intentions to progress.

Reframe the friction to present itself when avoiding your new identity, not acting in line with the new you. By this, I mean many people see getting up early to go to the gym as friction. They see taking time out of the day to meditate as friction and cooking a healthy meal as friction. As I stated earlier, humans naturally gravitate toward comfort, so change your mindset to place the discomfort zone as the *new you*, and the discomfort lies beyond whenever you are tempted to revert back to old habits (pull out a cigarette, open up the UberEATS app, drive past the gym). This is also known as your conscience or gut telling you that you know what you *should* be doing, so don't give into the temptation of the old you trying to pull you back to old habits. If you battle with this regularly when trying to make a change, props for progression can be used effectively.

ACCOUNTABILITY

In terms of keeping yourself accountable, there are three ways in which you can do this. First of all, you can be self-accountable. This is the most effective yet most difficult form of accountability because you truly have to be honest with yourself. You have to feel guilty when you skip a workout, have your conscience select the correct choice when debating spending money on frivolous items, and choosing to cook a nutritious meal over ordering fast food. Even at times when you want to treat yourself (maybe as a progress prop, for example), you need to be meticulous and plan rewards and not mistake them as lapses in habits.

The second form of accountability is finding an accountability partner. I like to call it "a moving buddy" in reference to the 1996 movie *Toy Story*. A moving buddy is one who checks in with you to make sure you are on track, as well as being the person who is both brutally honest with you and also your biggest fan. Your moving buddy keeps you accountable on a regular basis. This could be in a pact, which many people have in terms of a fitness goal, or just come from a detached outsider who can look at your progress objectively and deliver clarity on where you are at when you most need it.

The final form of accountability is in a group setting. This form works best when you find it difficult to hold yourself accountable, and it is why it is so helpful for people battling addiction such as "Alcoholics Anonymous" or making drastic changes in their life such as a weight-loss group. These groups are useful because the pressure of making sure you maintain the same track of progress as others are there, and for many, the fear of falling behind the group drives people to make their targets each week. The downside to this is you lose that personal touch a moving buddy has, and your goals may not be in a similar league to what other people want to do. There is also the aspect of time, and everyone undergoes their *Purpose Cycles* at different times and for different durations. You could have a *Purpose Cycle* that lasts you ten years, and group accountability can't fit in with that mold.

In reality, the only person who knows you the best is you. Therefore, you need to develop yourself to keep yourself accountable, but maybe with a little help from a moving buddy. You could also use journaling, checking in with your social media, or vlogging your progress to use an element of the group accountability as you will feel you have to keep pleasing your followers. These tools are all excellent ways of establishing a framework of accountability in your life. What's next is to deliver what you intend to do.

My toxic trait in previous *Purpose Cycles* was to think my moving buddies or accountability groups all doubted me, which gave me the spite I preached against earlier on in this section. This isn't a positive way to look at a goal, as you will always be acting on your intentions to seek external gratification. The best way to develop your self-accountability is to understand 90 percent of the time nobody will actually care what you do with your life. The only person it will affect is you. So, take charge, take the leap of faith, and be confident in what you are doing.

DISCIPLINE

Now that you have taken that first step, you will feel great about yourself. This is a reincarnation of you—not necessarily a different you—one who is an improved, best possible version of yourself. With each and every minute you spend enforcing these habits, momentum is building. The only thing about momentum is it can be rocked by a momentary lapse in finances, a family bereavement, or an unexpected result. So use this momentum as fuel; use it to ingrain these habits deep into your subconscious. Remember, setbacks refine you, not define you. They will ultimately etch a part of your personality with the lessons they teach you, as long as you use the value of a setback effectively.

The main misconception of the *Initiation* process is many people believe motivation is the fuel. Quite the contrary, as I mentioned in the *"Aspiration"* chapter. Motivation merely starts the engine.

You need *discipline* to show up day in, day out. There will be days when you feel flat, days when you want to put your early moves off to another day—purely because it is not yet an established habit. The discipline you show in your infancy of the *Purpose Cycle* pays dividends in the *Creation* and *Fruition* stages. "How does discipline form?" I hear you ask. It forms when you identify yourself with a set of habits and values that paint the picture of the person you want to be.

King of discipline, David Goggins states in his best-selling book *Can't Hurt Me* that the way to build discipline is by going through adversity. By doing things you don't want to do, you become more resilient. He says, "Difficulties and hardships are generally feared and avoided, but by reasoning this way, you risk missing out on your life. You will never discover your potential if you don't force it to reveal itself."

Goggins is well-renowned by many personal development fanatics as somebody who doesn't shy from a challenge. He preaches to his readers that putting yourself through "suffering" brings out the best of your potential. I know the word "suffering" is a bit extreme, but there is substance to his message. How much better do you feel after forcing yourself through an uncomfortable situation while coming out better on the other side? A way in which I test myself each day is I start the day by doing something I know I don't like: taking a cold shower. This gets my mind focused because I know it will be uncomfortable, but if I can get through those couple of minutes of pain every morning, I know I can face any challenge that day.

In your morning routine, it is important to build momentum. So do that uncomfortable task *early* to set the tone for the day. If you go against your new identity first thing in the morning by defying your challenge, then that also sets a precedent—a negative one.

The incredible aspect about discipline is it is the single most important weapon in your arsenal as you continue to move forward in your journey. Most people only identify with discipline when they need it the most. For example, it is cold and rainy outside, but staying indoors and not running is not part of the identity you want to uphold. Therefore you go out running anyway despite not wanting to.

CHAPTER 9

Tasks

TASK 6—IDENTIFY YOUR HABITS

For this task, you are going to keep a diary of your habits over the course of two weeks. The reason for the fortnight block is due to it ruling out a particularly unusual week or spontaneous event providing skewed data. The aim of this task is to ultimately review your day-to-day habits and realize how much time you spend doing various habits. Want a truly honest approach? If you live with somebody, ask them to document your habits. You may even end up surprised!

Document your habits for fourteen days in a table with the following columns:

Day:

Time:

Habit:

Duration spent on habit:

Ask one of your "fountains" close to you, "Do you think I spend too much time on a particular habit? What areas of my life could I be more productive in?" From the *Realization* stage, you will have already identified the fountains in your life, so in addition to a positive approach to this conversation, you should expect an honest answer that is designed to help you—not destroy your confidence.

Be sure not just to focus on the negatives. Ask the same friend, "What positive habits do I currently uphold that I can level up on? Which habits can I improve marginally to keep improving?"

Take note of your reflections:

I have noticed over the last two weeks _____
_____.

Upon completing this myself, I noticed a few bad habits:

- *I spent too much time on my phone.*
- *I spend* way *too much time on video games.*
- *My sleep suffered as a consequence of blue light exposure from the first two items.*
- *I often went "all in" with a new idea, hobby, or habit I wanted to form, just like many of us do with diets. I could not sustain said ideas because if you burn out an idea too quickly, you don't give it time to embed and establish itself within your routine. What I didn't plan for was a journey. I had the commitment to change, but I couldn't apply the consistency and conviction necessary.*

These reflections allowed me to figure out habits needed to be formed over time. Even when taking the initiative, it's important to start small and work your way up so you don't get overwhelmed and quit before you're through. When writing this book, I did not write the entire book over a week, I had to at first set time aside to write up to four hundred words each night, and then after a short period of time, I would pick up the laptop out of habit and write regardless. Whether it was two hundred words, or one thousand, I was writing.

This came from two things: one was the short burst of motivation to complete this book. It was something I had always wanted to do, and I had the motivation to complete the task, but I also had set a habit because on some days motivation can escape you. One twisted turn of events can make you feel like it is, "probably best to leave it today" or "you'll be fine if you skip it." If you set a habit, it becomes part of your identity. Therefore you don't end up thinking about accomplishing a task or not. You just do it.

James Clear talks about this further in *Atomic Habits*. He shows how 1 percent improvements across many different fields can make a huge impact over time. What is crucial from his message is that improvements are compounded over time, and we should not look for instant gratification. Now you are in the *Initiation* stage of your journey, it is crucial you don't expect instant gratification under any circumstances. It will not come to you.

Look at these facets of upgrading in life. Can you aspire to build yourself up by 1 percent each day in each block? Inevitably, this will lead to achieving your *Purpose*:

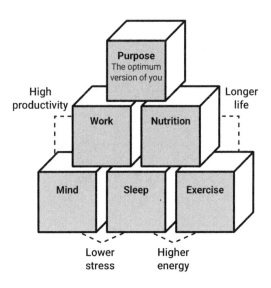

Fig. 3—Using these building blocks to find your *Purpose.*

On the outside of the diagram, you can see the results of excelling in two areas (higher energy, lower stress, etc.). A lot of people excel in one block of life, but most can probably identify with two they do well with. The hard part is excelling in more than two areas, which all support the top block: *Purpose.*

TASK 7—PROPS FOR PROGRESSION
If you are struggling to form a new habit, find yourself a reward to work toward. This sounds simple, but some people

feel like they need a progress prop to commence their journey. It is always nice to remind yourself you are doing a good job after starting a new habit. Even if you haven't achieved *Fruition*, starting is still a big step in the right direction.

Habit	Reward	Complete?
Go to the gym three times per week for two months.	New gym clothing I've always wanted from Gymshark.	Yes, I bought 2x T-shirts. Will add shorts after the next two months!

Use the example from the table above to complete five new habits you want to acquire, including your own props for progression! You could think about a prop for progression in each key area of your life. For example, have one for finance, one for diet, one for exercise, one for business, and so on.

The way I used the props during my timelines is I kept a scrapbook of my time in America. This acted as a constant reminder of the success I was having as the new me. I was keeping photos of the locations I was visiting, letters from the families I stayed with, and feedback I received. That way, if I ever missed my old routine, I would remind myself I'm doing great on my journey, so I shouldn't be tempted to revert back to comfort. Later on, in my journey at age twenty-five,

I purchased myself teaching essentials to suit my role in my new identity—stationery, a new shirt, etc. These props acted as reminders I am now an educator, not an unhappy business owner. These props acted as fuel to continue and made me so much more determined to succeed rather than fail and fall back to my old ways. In both of those stories, you've seen positive reinforcement.

In my twenty-eight timeline, I was fed up with looking for other people to blame for my problems. Although I was in a situation where I couldn't seem to catch a break, I knew I wanted to become somebody who took control of situations. I already had my own limiting beliefs, and adding to them by letting in the thoughts of others would only make things worse. Therefore, I used negative punishment to take away the props for progress if I blamed somebody else for what I was going through. I did this by simply not allowing myself to see my friends for drinks that weekend or "fine" myself money that was going into a savings account (this way, it was a win, win: I was reinforcing behavior while saving money long-term).

For each individual, *Initiation* will look different, but the one commonality is to take the leap to the new you. You must make this new you a part of your identity.

TASK 8—THE NEW IDENTITY

Think deeply about the finished "you" on this current *Purpose Cycle*, not the completed, fulfilled you (unless this is the *Purpose Cycle* later in life that delivers that). What does the future you who is reaping *Fruition* months, years, maybe decades from now look like after accomplishing their goals with the groundwork you are about to lay down?

On a piece of paper, jot a short description of what you pictured in the *Aspiration* phase. Your "*Fruition* You" may have been tweaked slightly following the *Realization* phase, but the principle is the same. The more you revisit, visualize, and realign your goals, the more likely you are to achieve them.

Think about these questions:

Why is this new you so appealing?

What adversities can you envision your new you to have gone through?

What skills have the "new you" obtained?

If you can answer these questions clearly, then you have a lot of clarity over what it is you are looking for.

Contrary to belief, it was, in fact, Will Durant in 1961, not Aristotle, who stated, "We are what we repeatedly do. Excellence then is not an act, but a habit." By now, you will have propelled yourself into a routine which is establishing itself in your subconscious. The dopamine rewards from following your routine and considering yourself successful in doing so will be *replacing* the props for progress (the negative punishment of guilt follows if otherwise), and you will consider it the norm to be doing the things you do day-to-day.

Kevin Dickinson wrote a fascinating article on participation medals in 2019. He highlights how participation medals devalue the meaning of "real awards," and I must say, I agree completely with him. He states, "Children aren't idiots. They understand not everybody is a winner and winning is better than losing. They're equally aware that a first-place trophy is more valuable than a participation trophy." To reward the child who came last but took part can apply to the version of you that is going through the motions. Props for progress, just like participation medals, are *not* for showing up. Both adults and children should be rewarded for their *effort*.

It is a feeling echoed by Dickinson, who goes on to say:

"Good practice seems to be giving younger children trophies, but ones that award effort, not just showing up. These trophies would praise individual merit and improvement—whether that's achieving a PR, improving a specific skill, or even something as simple as getting over a fear of the ball. For old children, it's best to drop the trophies altogether and replace them with praise for effort and growth in tandem with honest discussion on how to improve."

Do the same with yourself. Every time you reach a milestone, reward yourself with a prop for progression. In the meanwhile, remember to praise yourself. You're improving every day!

LESSONS LEARNED FROM *INITIATION*:
1. **It doesn't matter where and when you begin acting on your ambitions. The important thing is you actually**

take that first step. Your first podcast will be crap, your first article will be crap, your first workout, business pitch, and public speech will be crap! That is by no means a put-down. It is just a fact because one day, you will look back on those *necessary* first attempts and reflect on how far you've come since then. After all, the worst attempt is the one you never did.

2. **Developing a habit is key to establishing a routine and ultimately embedding a new identity and progress toward your goals.** To embed this habit, you must repeat the action(s) consistently over a period of time. Maybe even an external use of a prop for progression can help you take the steps required before you develop an internal belief that this is a part of your identity.

3. **Accountability is going to play a *huge* part in your journey.** Set up your systems early with accountability partners and use props for progression effectively. Once you get to the stage of building self-discipline, you will be in a positive habit.

Three lessons I've learned about myself from **Initiation** *is:*

1.
2.
3.

Key Character trait: **Discipline**

PART 4

CREATION

CHAPTER 10

Research, Strategize, Act

22

At this point, I was living the life I wanted to live to build success. I had a routine set of regularly working out, driving to each venue of my work for the day, delivering high-quality football coaching, and then heading back to my host family for a nice home-cooked meal. Life was good. Responsibilities were low, and I could just focus on being me. There were no university social groups to adhere to, no petty relationships back home, and I was purely myself. I can honestly look back and say that was a true turning point in my life.

I took the opportunity to educate myself. This was my first vivid memory of my three main steps of *Creation: Research, Strategize, Act*. I conducted my *Research* with audiobooks, actual books, and just talking to people who have life experience. Some of the stories I accumulated from the various families I stayed with were fascinating, especially one family in particular: the DeLeeuws.

My opening months in the US were amazing. I was living as a new, upgraded version of me. I had struggled to find a place to stay for that particular week because there was some downtime. However, the DeLeeuws stepped in. Candice, the host mother, had approached me to ask if I still needed a place a few weeks back, which I did. After work had finished for the day, I drove back to the neighborhood in tandem with Candice. As I gazed around my new street for the week, I witnessed a purely breathtaking view.

It was like what I saw on US television programs: a suburban paradise of a street with children cycling with their families past the huge houses, endless conjoined back yards with trees reaching up to decorate the landscape further. The sheer beauty of the place was accompanied by the soundtrack of enough birds to serenade the neighborhood without overstepping their presence. Pulling up into the drive, I was greeted by Brandon, the host-father. Tall, charismatic, he was the model dad.

Could this be a new Aspiration? I pondered, looking around at the life Brandon and Candice had crafted: a loving family, beautiful house, successful careers. It seemed to be a life without limits.

Upon getting to know the DeLeeuw family further, I understood this had not come without its own challenges. Candice DeLeeuw was already, in my eyes, a strong mother. She and her husband Brandon had an incredible aura of kindness about them. I also noticed how strong they were as a couple, with a connection I could only aspire to have once I met the person I was supposed to be with. When they told me the story of how they had begun dating and then, within a matter of months, got married and moved halfway across the country to pursue a new job, I was amazed by how deeply they fell in love and made such colossal life choices. They then told me a story of their past which shook me to the core.

Not long after they were married, Candice gave birth to Alexander, a beautiful baby boy. Candice also told this story in her own book, *Hope (Amidst the Stories I Told Myself)* (DeLeeuw, 2021). She writes about how she had felt an unease in the events leading up to Alexander's birth. There were several signs which she came to understand were messages from God of what could potentially happen, signs such as stumbling across a children's cemetery or being asked about taking up ICU insurance. She had prayed upon arrival at the hospital and reflected on this experience as "Messages from God."

At that moment in time, she had no idea what she and her family were about to endure, for the two young lovers who had been swept up in a whirlwind of romance Candice herself described as "Danny and Sandy's summer fling." It transpired that the relationship they had dived into head-first was soon to be strained with the pressures that came with having their firstborn go through open-heart surgery just days after his birth. It was a parent's worst nightmare.

Many weeks had passed, and in Candice's book, she talks about staying up in the family accommodation on her own to be with Alex as much as she could be. When it became apparent Alexander was potentially going to lose his life, Candice had found solitude in praying in the hospital corridor. Much to her surprise, she received a message from God and an overwhelming calm and understanding of what his plan was for her little boy.

Candice referred to a particular moment when she and her husband agreed to only keep their son on life support if he was going to have a life. By that, she meant they were not going to have Alexander on life support if he wasn't able to live a life without pain. Candice referred to a moment in which Alexander was taken off support and he was left to breathe independently—something he hadn't done since he had just been born. Candice and Brandon held Alexander as he took his final breaths on Earth.

In those final moments of Alexander's life, Candice referred to Alexander's last breath not being "frightening or gasping. It was like a sigh of relief. A sigh of relief from all of the pain he had experienced during all those weeks."

Candice wrote so bravely and incredibly in her book.

The book helped me deal with my own grief, which I was yet to suffer until the twenty-three timeline, and allowed me to process what I was going through. The *Creation* phase is ultimately about becoming a well-rounded version of *you*. Therefore, being able to resonate with the experiences of my American family is something I will never forget.

I cannot even begin to imagine the unfathomable reality of losing a child. I have written earlier about my experience of losing one of my closest friends, and with that, I have felt an overwhelming amount of appreciation for having met the DeLeeuw family. They have taught me so many valuable lessons about how to cope with loss, how to cope with the heartache, how to cope with the emptiness that is left when someone is taken away from you, and how to cope with using love and positivity to rebuild your life—when it feels completely broken.

To think my experience with the DeLeeuw family was only a year before I had lost my friend—to a heart condition, may I add—was strangely coincidental. It appears life somehow throws signals at you in the form of people, situations, environments, and experiences. Fate often determines what life has set out for us. We can attempt to pave ourselves a path in which we want to live, but the only true choice we have is what we put out in terms of the universe and how we react to what the universe gives back. It is not always a fair deal, but you will never be given something you're not strong enough to handle.

Within my American routine, I had gathered the basic information on how a successful coaching business was run. I immersed myself in the day-to-day running my bosses, Ben and Mel, were grinding out during the *Research* phase, and I understood the foundations they had laid years ago were now paying dividends, in more ways than one.

I now had to *Strategize* how I was going to implement, or more specifically *recreate*, the life I have here in the UK. During my evenings, I would spend time with the host family, relax, revise my plans for the next day, and then just before I went to sleep, I would get out the notebook and make additions to the business plan. As the months grew shorter, I was becoming more and more apprehensive about taking such a huge step at twenty-three. After all, I knew although I had gathered a great deal of intelligence around how the company was operated, I did not have a clue how the accounts were run, the advertisement behind it, and so much more. I was a sports coach—a good one, but still a sports coach.

I knew my limits and needed to address them. In the meanwhile, I was focused on doing what I did know to the best of my ability. I began to formulate my coaching programs of what I would be offering once I landed back in England—the *Creation* phase was well and truly underway. What I managed to do was apply the three main steps of the *Creation* phase: *Research, Strategize,* and now I had to *Act.*

25

At the age of twenty-five, I felt like the experiences of the business, then training to be a teacher gave me a huge amount of life experience. I felt an overwhelming feeling of fulfillment. I had secured a role in teaching! *Purpose Cycle* complete? The danger is we often get to that goal and "take the foot off the gas."

I wasn't yet qualified. I was merely a student, and that summer, I had read many different articles about becoming a new teacher: the challenges that lay ahead, the endless hours of marking, the amazing inner feeling when a student had the "lightbulb moment." I also made sure I was well-prepared. I had bought a diary and had planned out my weeks in advance (naive, I know! I was yet to discover how unpredictable becoming a schoolteacher really was with each day presenting the unknown). However, it felt real as I was embarking on a path of discovery. This wasn't the unknown, so I couldn't label it "fear of the unknown"; the preparation I had done that summer was to eradicate that very possibility. The only fear I had was the fear of remaining average—and that was the fuel that drove me to work on my first day as a student teacher.

The school I was based in was fantastic. I will always appreciate the start they gave me in the profession. I already knew the staff from my sports business in the previous years, but this was different. I was in the classroom now and looking to inspire my own set of students. As I took my final stride onto the steps of the school, an overwhelming feeling oozed its way around my limbs—impostor syndrome!

Impostor syndrome is essentially an overwhelming inner emotion of not feeling as if you belong in the situation you find yourself in. When some people succeed in life, they wonder why it was them who actually reached their goal. It is common among people who visualize and manifest their goals, work really hard to achieve them but have low self-esteem. Impostor syndrome essentially derives from limiting beliefs placed from others into our own minds.

Abigail Abrams, in a 2018 *Time* article, debunks a common misconception that only people with low self-esteem suffer from impostor syndrome. Perfectionists are also affected because they question their own competence if they are not successful with their vision. Naturally, high achievers also suffer from this in a new environment due to their expectation of always being the smartest person in the room and not wanting to look otherwise. Abrams goes on to say, "An estimated 70 percent of people experience these impostor feelings at some point in their lives."

These people often ask, "Why me?" when they should be acknowledging the fact that they put out their affirmations and vibrations of what they wanted to achieve by visualizing their goals, speaking their goals, and then working hard. It should come as no surprise to them that they are successful, yet it still occurs. Take a lesson from famous mixed martial artist Conor McGregor. He stated after his historic win in UFC 194 over Jose Aldo in 2015, "If you can see it here (points to head), and you have the courage enough to speak it. It will happen." It is that level of assurance and execution of the Law of Attraction that should eradicate all feelings of impostor syndrome.

It wasn't until I had acknowledged these feelings' existence and processed them that I was able to function that morning. I believe emotional intelligence is more than just having a cry and "expressing your emotions." It is truly understanding them, processing them correctly, and then harnessing them to your advantage, which is exactly what I did that day.

I reflected back and thought to myself, *I wanted this. I visualized myself in a classroom inspiring young minds. I deserve to be here because, despite being written off in Sixth Form, despite being written off at university, I had the courage to verbalize my dreams. I made sure they became a reality.*

I knew these feelings were natural, and my mind wanted me to revert to the convenience and comfort of a low-challenge life. I was not prepared to let my mind win. For me,

I was battling two fears: the fear of failure and the fear of remaining average. In reality, the fear of remaining average was a lot more daunting than it was to try something and fail. So, I took a deep breath, told myself I deserved this opportunity and the dream wasn't accomplished yet, and made the fear serve me as a fountain rather than drain my energy for the day.

As former special forces operative and author Ant Middleton stated in *The Fear Bubble in 2020*, "You can either make fear work for you or against you." I raced into my new classroom. I knew if I stopped to take a breath, that would be it. The fear would consume me, and I would hesitate in every aspect of performing my duties that day.

I sat down in my seat and took five slow, deep breaths, and questioned myself: 1.What was I actually afraid of? 2.Who actually cares if I begin my career as the best or the worst teacher on the planet? I'll only get better, and the world won't end. 3.Why am I linking all of these external factors to my fear? I cannot affect them. 4.My own insecurities are the reason I am feeling like this. What perceived weaknesses do I have to confront in order to succeed today? 5. How am I going to make today a great opportunity to learn and grow?

Relax.

I opened my eyes. Any of my new colleagues who might have walked past would have assumed I was some yoga-crazy nervous wreck of a teacher. In that individual moment, I discovered something profound: my fear became my energy, and it still is to this day.

Although each day I find myself becoming comfortable with once-labeled "difficult challenges," I find new challenges each day to deliver that same buzz I had on that very first day. A lot of people let their emotions consume them, and anxiety can do that, but this was a way I managed to control my fight or flight reactions—and it set me up for the rest of the day, term, and even year.

In the case of this particular anecdote, it just goes to show sometimes, no matter how much researching and strategizing you do, there will always be occasions where emotions take over, and you have to be adaptable in your thinking to strategize for those moments. "The plan for going off-plan," I call it. Be prepared for those scenarios because they can occur when you feel the most prepared you have ever felt, and they won't be anywhere to be seen when you aren't at all prepared. That's just how life works sometimes!

28

Being back loving what I do almost felt like *Fruition* itself, but I know becoming that new "Mike" was ever closer. As you enter new environments, new mentors emerge. The wonderful aspect of growth is you meet like-minded people with the energy you give out to the universe.

I had only been in my new workplace a matter of months, but I was already learning from so many people. To know you are living in accordance with your *Purpose* is one thing but understanding there will always be somebody who can mentor you and provide guidance is *true strength*. To assume an "I can take it from here" attitude is not going to help you reach your potential. That is why we should never be truly satisfied until we have experienced many *Purpose Cycles*.

The fear of failure I had experienced on my first day of teaching was creeping up on me. It felt like my last shot at working in education. I remembered the energy those feelings produced could be channeled into excitement and momentum as long as I followed the three main steps of *Creation*.

To be a successful teacher, researching my field was crucial. Starting this new challenge in this new environment meant I had to be well-prepared. I was viewing this new position as my last chance in the teaching game.

As I had previously mentioned, making a fresh start in the police and the Royal Air Force (RAF) deviated my attention. This was a new *Realization* for me; I had a false *Aspiration*. After only two years in the profession, I'd let the opinions of one person engulf my self-perception.

It's important to become objective in situations like this because you can either live in denial of what they are saying or do the opposite: take that person's opinion as gospel and let it become your identity, almost like a self-fulfilling prophecy. I had to dig deep and understand why I found it so difficult to connect with my previous environment. I had to ask myself the difficult question I asked in the *Realization* phase: "What can I do to ensure that situation doesn't happen again?"

This timeline is largely themed on second chances in a *Purpose Cycle*. Thankfully, this lifeline was handed to me. I had to prove I was a capable teacher whose prowess matched his ambitions. My second chance came from taking ownership of my situation and not blaming others. After all, the only person who could control my destiny was *me*.

The *Research* stage came long before I started in my new workplace. I had armed myself with the knowledge and skills to be successful. Many people fail to do this as they believe their first day is the day they first walk into the workplace. I wanted to enter on day one and bring innovative ideas into the workplace while being able to back myself in becoming an inspiring leader like Mike had done for me a couple of years prior. The hunger to become an expert in a field I considered a weakness (teaching technology) was pivotal to this growth. Evolution is part of the workplace, and there will always be new innovations that make their way into a professional environment. Rising to the top is not the hard part for successful people, it is keeping on top of the game. I wanted to adopt the mindset early on in my career that I will always be a learner.

A month to the day before my first official day at work, I scribed a six-page strategy on how I would make an impact in my role as technology lead and class teacher. This was more for me than anything. I would strongly recommend anybody who is starting a new challenge to complete a road map to success. I started it by laying out the parameters in which I would judge myself and what I thought my superiors would judge me on. I had to uphold these standards to the highest level and had to back up each parameter with an array of evidence to prove I could adhere to what I had set myself prior to the new school year beginning. I had given myself targets in areas such as: results from my class, my ability to lead, providing professional development for others, and my own professional growth (enrolling in further courses).

This can apply to any workplace, and I was so glad I had enforced this on myself before starting. It gave me a clear vision of how I envisioned myself as a success, and I could also reflect on each goal and tweak them if necessary. Hold yourself accountable first and foremost. I now do this going into every school year. Yes, the document is personal to me, but it is also essential evidence if I want to go into any form of progression meeting. If you're going into a meeting with your boss to discuss progression in the company, then arming yourself with a professional development strategy is a great way to showcase your value.

Ramit Sethi from the book *I Will Teach You to Be Rich* calls this "The briefcase effect." Preparing yourself for these meetings with evidence of high performance in your role is essential when discussing progression with your bosses. I also had the gift of becoming a reflective person from my past experience. It awarded me criteria in which I felt were valuable, I wasn't a defensive person anymore, and I gave my all to the role and worked for something far greater than myself. Buying into your *Purpose* allows you to emotionally invest in your role, and you will naturally perform better. This is also simply defined as "passion."

So, who my former employers perceived as a failure was now a highly valuable part of a company—or at least I now felt valued. To many people in the profession who were superior to my role, I may have looked somewhat over-prepared for my first weeks in the job, but I can guarantee you the employee who is over-prepared 99 percent of the time walks out in higher esteem than the average worker. It's a chicken/egg scenario: being well-prepared drives people's belief in you, which then further spurs you on!

I followed this newbie momentum by spending the year implementing what I had strategized in the months leading up to beginning the role. Backing up what you say is somewhat difficult, especially to me. This is why I made it into an official document. It was there printed in black and white, and I couldn't walk away from it. Telling yourself, "I'll go to the gym tomorrow morning," is an easily breakable promise, but documenting a road map on how you are going to be successful is a promise your conscious mind will endeavor to keep. Just like the Conor McGregor quote from earlier, "If you have the courage to speak it, then it will happen."

James Clear in *Atomic Habits* calls this an "Implementation Intention." This is a statement that you are going to do something to support the cause you are trying to achieve.

If this is a dream you, in the form of a healthier you, the implementation intention may go along the lines of, "If the weather is dry tomorrow, I will walk rather than taking the bus to work." This shows you are intent on doing so and is a great place to start.

However, it does leave a little room for a lack of execution. What if it starts spitting ever-so-slightly with rain? Intention failed! I prefer to be very specific, like saying, "I will attend the gym on Mondays, Wednesdays, and Fridays at 5:30 a.m."

Boom! Contract locked in. Try writing down your personal road map to success, as well as your professional one. Holding yourself accountable in all areas of your life will set in stone the systems and habits that will define the person who will be achieving their true *Fruition*.

These intentions feel incredible as they make you verbalize what you are going to do to achieve. Each time you execute an implementation intention, celebrate it! You are a doer, not a talker! There are too many talkers in this world, so don't go around blurting out implementation intentions; write them down and journal for yourself. Also, remember: *Research, Strategize, Act, Reflect, Repeat.* In the next section, we will dive into the meanings behind these steps of *Creation*.

CHAPTER 11

Embodying *Fruition*

———

Creation is the day-to-day life you now live. During the previous stages, you constructed your new identity. *Creation* is about following that identity. The end goal within you is what drives you, but habits are what ultimately fuels your success.

In the *Realization* phase, you identified negative habits and curated positive habits to craft the identity of the new you. The reason I identify this person as the "new you" rather than the "future you" is because you need to start living it *now*. Many people use the phrase, "Fake it until you make it," and while I like the thought behind it, you are by no means faking it. You are living it, and each day you act in line with the "new you" is more fuel in the tank that will carry you to *Fruition*. The three ways you can process *Creation* is: *research, strategize,* and *act.*

Acting in accordance with your own "dream-self" is critical to you achieving your dreams. It sounds obvious, but there are so many people who aspire to be greater but then continue with the same mindset, habits, and beliefs they have always had. If you want your life to change, then *you* need to change.

For some, small changes could be all that is required. For others, it'll be a case of making huge lifestyle shifts. Regardless, we began to visualize and manifest our dream lives in the *Aspiration* phase. Therefore we must act in accordance with that person we visualized in the movie theater.

If you're like me and you require regular bouts of reassurance that what you're doing is on the right path, then taking the steps you have taken in this book just proves how far you have come. While it's important to feel good about taking a step forward each day toward success, understand not every day will feel like it is a step forward. When things get hard, here's what you do: trust the process. Always understand you are making progress (we will dive into this shortly when I introduce IMPACT ideas). There will be bumps in the road, wrong turns, and cul-de-sacs, but what is vital during these challenges is that you review, reflect, and redirect yourself back on the path to success.

There will also inevitably be doubters. The more successful you become, the more doubters you will acquire—it's a fact. A quote from one of my all-time favorite films, *The Pursuit of Happyness* from 2006, resonates with me when I feel defensive of my goals:

"You got a dream… You gotta protect it. People can't do somethin' themselves, they wanna tell you, you can't do it. If you want something, go get it. Period."

It is also important to understand that as long as you are doing something right, people will mock you or try and knock you down. "Tall Poppy Syndrome" is used commonly in Australia or New Zealand as a slang term for when other people try to climb higher than their peers and are ridiculed, canceled, or cut down because of it.

The reference to the poppies is they should all grow in uniform, and no poppy should stand taller than the other. An article on *Women of Influence* by Dr. Rumeet Billan and Todd Humber in 2018 showed that from the sample of 1,501 people drawn across numerous industries and organizations, 87.3 percent stated their achievements at work were undermined by colleagues or superiors. Furthermore, more than 81 percent said they had experienced hostility or were penalized because of their success. This included unfair treatment in the workplace, bosses ostracizing them from their colleagues, or purposely overlooking them for promotions. What is alarming is those are the figures of people we are aware of who undermine us, never mind those who go behind our backs when we take strides toward personal achievement.

This speaks volumes about the insecurities of others. Never take the insults or hostility personally; your achievements highlight their lack of action. To understand their way of thinking further, I would like you to think back to a time where you may have shown jealousy toward a partner, a former colleague, or a friend. Why did you feel that way? What did their strengths highlight in your weaknesses? Did you do something about your own weaknesses? Or did you blame/ ridicule the person who achieved something? What can you do next time to *research, strategize,* and *act*? Those three steps all point to *you*. It is about taking full and complete responsibility for your pathway to success. It starts by becoming a worthy rival.

BECOME THE WORTHY RIVAL

A contributing factor toward impostor syndrome is the perception we will be treated like the tall poppies, not the giant bamboo that has put so much hard work into getting where you want to in life. However, we need to reframe this perception once again: from impostor, to worthy rival.

In his book *The Infinite Game,* Simon Sinek talks about a worthy rival being, "Other players in the game worthy of comparison. Studying them reveals to us our opportunities to improve so we can remain players in the game and better advance our Just Cause."

Sinek states rather than trying to beat our competition, we should learn about ourselves from understanding how their strengths are our weaknesses, and our strengths are probably their weaknesses—because more often than not, your rivals probably feel the same about you too.

This is something I can hand-on-heart admit I used to fall into. I used to resent the fact I had a rival, or somebody who was striving for the same thing as me, so much to the point that while it made me produce results, it was at the expense of relationships or external validation. To achieve true long-term success, happiness, and fulfillment, you must acknowledge rivals are a healthy part of your life. To champion their successes makes you a team player and a great person, not a weak person who just lets other people win. You can be happy for someone while aspiring to what they have achieved. This is different from envy, which has more of a negative connotation.

To gain a clear structure for your *Creation* phase, learning regularly via research, planning a strategy for success, and then acting on those promises you have made to yourself is the way to true success. To break this down further, you can ensure your day-to-day action carries IMPACT.

DEVELOPING IMPACT IDEAS

An IMPACT idea is a huge step of the *Creation* phase. This is how you are going to move forward and evolve. The aim of all *Purpose Cycles* is to finish the cycle better than when you entered, and a way of strategizing your way to a greater life is to develop an IMPACT idea.

WHAT IS AN IMPACT IDEA?

I—Innovative
M—Measurable
P—Positive
A—Accountable
C—Conviction
T—Trust

I—INNOVATIVE

All ideas and aspirations stem from experiences and beliefs we already have. An example of this is seeing a computer and wanting to build a tech company, having a bad experience when purchasing a dress and launching your own fashion brand, or even positive experiences like completing a fitness journey and subsequently aspiring to become a personal trainer.

The key to having IMPACT with your idea is making sure it is innovative—this could be a brand-new creation within a field, or it could be a niche within a niche! The more creative, useful, and niche your idea is, the more likely it is to succeed. The trick here is you never get asked the question, "So what?" Your idea will already answer those questions when people see the direction you are taking it.

M—MEASURABLE

Similar to those who are used to setting S.M.A.R.T goals, having an idea that is measurable is a huge way to measure success but also manage your time effectively. The first thing to measure is your timescale. Is your *Purpose Cycle* a microcycle (short-term)? Is it a mesocycle (medium-term?)? Or is it a macrocycle (long-term)? Once you establish a set time frame, you will be able to focus accordingly.

For example: I wanted to become a better speaker, so I applied for a speaking gig that was three months away. Once I got the gig, I enrolled in a public speaking online course. This helped me plan the timescale for the *Research* phase (planning the content of my presentation), I then used the tools from the course to assist with my delivery (the *Strategy* phase), and three months after I started my microcycle, I delivered my presentation (the *Act* phase).

Other ways you can measure your idea is to use the metrics associated with your idea: If it's a fitness goal, you will use the weights you are lifting, your 5K time, or your weight to measure how you are performing in alignment to your goal. If it is a business you have started, you will measure the customer engagement and the income you are gaining from the business.

P—POSITIVE

Positivity and optimism are often misconstrued as "blind happiness." This is because positive people are often seen online as successful people who are only smiling because things are going right for them. This is so far off the mark it's unreal.

Positivity is understanding the situation that is in front of you and choosing to respond in a manner that will serve you. It is a matter of life that you will not always have the rub of the green, but this isn't to say that you should moan about it. The way I see positivity is like a phone battery. If you never charge it (by reading books, exercising, hydrating, journaling, and meditation, for example), you will eventually run out or hit a low point when situations (or people) are constantly taking from you. Therefore, it is important to keep charging your positivity up because when things do take from your battery, you are able to remain at a high level and recharge back to full.

Hard-hitting events in particular really do test our positive thinking, such as losing money in an investment, illness, or loss of loved ones, and not getting the job we had hoped for, which is why we need to do all we can to keep the levels as high as we can. When these events do come around, it will take a while to charge back to full.

If you approach your idea with a growth mindset and understand things may (and probably will) go wrong from time to time, this is a process, and if we learn failure ultimately serves us, then we will become much happier and much more positive.

A—ACCOUNTABLE

Being accountable is what separates successful people from the average Joe. The most successful people in life are constantly looking at themselves and where they can improve. Yes, they also look at people around them, but they own their circumstances and understand they may need to change or adjust their circle to succeed.

An accountability buddy is a great way to begin a process. I had touched on this previously when I mentioned obtaining a "moving buddy" to build accountability. I love this example because we can choose our own moving buddies who help us move forward toward our goals. The goals between the two could be aligned (such as a gym partner), or they could be there in a supportive role (reading a manuscript for a book).

The greatest part of having an accountability partner is being comfortable enough to admit to your partner that you are finding your journey tough. Having that person to "lean on" is just as important as somebody keeping you on track by giving you "tough love." I believe humans aren't as effective at communicating as we were even twenty years ago—despite having ample support networks in the forms of therapy, family, friends, and partners. Technology, "ghosting culture," and lack of face-to-face interaction are damaging our relationships.

Dougherty supports this in a 2013 blog article by stating:

"Because we rely on our technology, we lack the relationships that are created through speaking to others, causing a lack of experience in the ability to communicate maturely with others. The ability to make friends outside of "friend requesting" them on a social media site decreases because the ability to communicate outside of the technological world is lost."

Dougherty goes on to explain this in his article by saying, "The level of face-to-face interaction and conversation has decreased because of this new best friendlike relationship with our technology. Instead of meeting up with someone to talk things out, we simply shoot them a text, and in a matter of seconds, we have a response." To build those communication and interaction skills, I suggest group accountability.

Group accountability is a positive step forward to being successful. Look at Slimming World as an example—nobody wants to let the tribe down. I see group accountability as a great way to begin and feed off successful people and their habits. Both methods of accountability are not sustainable if the most important person in the process doesn't look at their own being and put them at the forefront of accountability.

Ultimately, it is down to you.

Ask yourself a difficult question every day, see yourself grow, understand you are a person who sets yourself a promise and they stick to it, and you will see results.

C—CONVICTION

You may see a lot of Instagram pages that have been set up without a post since "May 2015" or a new business idea that is a flash in the pan but nowhere to be seen months down the line. If you are not consistent with your idea and don't implement it with conviction, then ultimately, your idea will fail.

If your goal is "I want to lose ten pounds," and all you do is go to the gym once a week for twenty minutes, you will not make much difference. If you look at your diet, your hydration, your NEAT (calories burned while in a nonexercise state), and you go to the gym, even if it is once a week, then you will start to notice a difference. Conviction is what kills the majority of ideas, as most people aren't willing to put in the reps to be successful.

Write down the characteristics of a successful you ten years down the line. Is this person resilient? Is this person consistent? Is this person adaptable? Then there's your answer, put in the work now and consistently, then you will see the change you desire.

T—TRUST

This is a journey you are on. Life itself is a process. It could be classed as a macro-*Purpose Cycle*. You must apply all of the above and trust this will work for you to see the results you desire. Knowing there will be bumps in the road is a part of everyday life. Investing yourself fully in becoming a better you, despite outcomes not going your way all of the time should be expected on your *Purpose Cycle*. The key word is *yet*—I'm not there *yet*, but I will be one day.

Connie Mathers builds on this with her 2021 article, "Trust the Process: 8 Ways to Use This Mantra in Your Life." She says we should "Learn to be happy in the present moment without rushing to meet a final goal. Be willing to be flexible and go with the flow. Learn to accept uncertainty—but always be certain that you can find growth in your struggles."

The flexibility to allow uncertainty to happen because you are certain you will grow really struck me. Uncertainty can often derail dreams. When you can visualize your success, you know it will still happen for you.

I enjoy visualizing and manifesting my dream life. This keeps me grounded. I understand I am nowhere near that stage yet, and I need to continue pushing for my goals, but it helps me reflect because I see the future me, and I compare him with the person I am now. If I am not acting in accordance with that identity, then I need to revise my habits.

This is a process, and mistakes will occur along the way. Obstacles will present themselves to you, and you must trust this will ultimately make you a stronger, more refined person in the long run. Enjoy the Cycle and see where you are going to be if you remain consistent and true to yourself. How can you adopt the IMPACT idea structure? It could be for a side project, a way to obtain a promotion at work or a way to improve your health and well-being.

RESISTANCE TO EXTERNAL FACTORS

Creation is essentially the day-to-day "hustle." How you fill these days add up as compound interest to your own personal development. So, when you are faced with decisions that will either benefit you in the long-term but not the short-term (delayed gratification) or benefit you now but not in the long-term (instant gratification), say to yourself, "What would future me think if I chose this path?"

Bear this in mind at the forefront of all decision-making. There will always be moments when your willpower is tested: the bed seems so warm and comfy, the smell of McDonald's fast food is luring you in as you drive past, and the staff at the store are upselling the chocolate bars (it feels like they're doing it intentionally to test you, doesn't it?). I now relish these moments throughout the day because I understand my environment is always going to challenge me, my social circles are always going to challenge me, and my own limiting beliefs are always going to test me. Reframe this from "These external factors just don't understand what I'm going through" to "I enjoy the fact these elements are keeping me accountable and reminding me why I'm on this journey."

In each moment you are tested, you will be faced with a decision, and more often than not, the easy decision is the one that will hurt you in the long-term. There have been times while writing this book where I have had to face these decisions: at this very moment of writing these words, the sun is shining beautifully, and people are flocking to the beer gardens of East Yorkshire. It would be incredibly easy for me to join them, but I know in the future I would kick myself if I looked back and this book wasn't finished.

As you evolve through this journey, you will banish many limiting beliefs that haunted you in the early stages, but there will always be that voice that will test you, whether it is your former self or the voice of others who have stuck with you. I want you to acknowledge that voice, relish that test of your new self, and go out there and prove that voice wrong. To reference the words of Naval Ravikant, "All self-help boils down to choosing long-term over short-term."

We now live in a world with a plethora of ways to deliver instant gratification to our lives. If we want to get somewhere fast, we order an Uber. If we don't want to cook, we order a takeaway. If we want to watch a movie, we go on Netflix. We can even go on a seventy-two-hour juice "cleanse" to feel like we're healthy enough to eat junk food for the rest of the month again.

Everything is readily available to us at the tap of a button or the wave of a bank card. Modern society has made us lazy as human beings, and the only way around it is to think long-term with every decision we make. As I mentioned earlier in previous sections, we all gravitate toward comfort and convenience, but convenience is the killer of all dreams to be great. When faced with these decisions, it is important to take a step back and look at the situation from an objective viewpoint. Remember *Good Will Hunting*—choose the hammer.

Deciding whether or not something brings you instant gratification is relatively simple: if it feels like temptation, then it should be considered to be avoided. That is your future you sounding the alarm bells to think longer-term. It will bring you a short burst of dopamine (the reward chemical) that burns like a flash in the pan. These hits of dopamine come in many different forms—according to a *Healthline.com* article by Erica Julson—but a common avenue people seek instant gratification from is social media.

These platforms are designed to provide short-burst dopamine hits with likes, comments, ads, and also liking others' content that gives you a sense of generosity as easy as double-tapping. Julson explains in her article, "—you can gain natural dopamine hits from eating healthy food, exercising regularly, and sleeping often."

These sources transform your life because it provides a greater quality of chemical that lasts longer. Consuming quick-gained, instant gratification dopamine can be dangerous if overly relied upon. Dopamine can be an addictive chemical, which is why those who are given technology so young or are new to the technology like many adults become addicted to smartphones. It's why those exposed to alcohol at a young age become more likely to be alcohol dependent, and that is why it is so easy to spiral into a negative and unhealthy state of living if all you chase is the quick-fix dopamine hits.

The three major happiness chemicals, according to an article titled "Essential Guide To Serotonin And The Other Happy Hormones In Your Body" on *Atlas Blog* are: Oxytocin (the chemical that stems from affection) by cuddling your dog, holding hands with your partner, seeing your family and giving a compliment; Serotonin (the chemical that affects your mood) by meditating, journaling, walking and sun exposure; Endorphins (the chemical that controls pain) by laughing, exercising, eating dark chocolate and spending time with friends.

Think of these chemicals as rich, organic foods that will provide your mental health with way greater results than seeking a short-term dopamine hit. Bottom line—put down the phone and be present with your friends and family!

DELAYED GRATIFICATION

Josh Beet is an online coach from my hometown of Kingston upon Hull. On a 2021 episode in *The Purpose Cycle Podcast*, he spoke about the life skills he had from something as simple as heading down to his local Blockbuster store during his childhood:

"I had to work hard at school to earn the right to choose a movie and had to negotiate with my sisters over which films to choose as we had a limit of three films. I had to make decisions that would impact my whole weekend, and these skills helped me switch from a convenient mindset to one that is meticulous and strategic."

Think back to your childhood at the moments that provide resistance, friction, and challenge. Choose the hammer.

As Josh states in the episode, "There's a subconscious side to us that thinks, 'I want to achieve X, I'm just going to go and do it.' But we kind of overlook that actually, this is going to be quite tough." Those experiences growing up have provided you with the foundation to want to take on a self-improvement journey. This is why these early childhood experiences are critical in forming our resilience for adulthood.

Social media prays on the weakness we have when we doubt we can climb the obstacles life throws in front of us. You see a lot of "make millions trading forex" sponsored posts or "lose two stone in four weeks" posts from influencers. All they ask you to do is pay for the course that will teach you exactly how to do it, but the courses cost more than what it would cost to invest in yourself long-term. It is human nature to want something quick, so quite often, people fall into this trap.

The way Josh works with his clients is to work with them (not for them) over the course of three months to build a framework to educate them on fitness, nutrition, and all-round physical and mental performance, rather than gain quick fixes, so they become a returning customer the following summer. Unfortunately, not all coaches and "influences" are like Josh, and they preach to gain fast results—that is how they sell their services. They prey on those people who lack the resilience to follow the three steps of *Creation*: *Research, Strategize, Act*.

When seeking help from coaches, make sure you find out their motives. You want sustainable results and an education—not a quick, unsustainable fix.

SEIZING OPPORTUNITIES YOU ATTRACT, NOT CHASE

Does this mean you should go out and search for gratification? I believe opportunities and situations will be attracted to you *if* you put the correct message out into the universe for it to do so. Bob Proctor in *You Were Born Rich* talks about the Law of Vibration:

"Attraction is a law, but it's the secondary law. The primary law is the law of vibration. The law of vibration is one of the basic laws of the universe. It decrees that everything moves, nothing rests, we literally live in an ocean of motion."

If you are a drain, a toxic person, such as someone who acts negatively to those around you, you might get bitter if somebody achieves at work, or you may get jealous or controlling if you see your partner talking to somebody of the opposite sex. You will attract toxic situations, or potentially situations that allow you to be that way inclined, such as being toxic to an undeserving partner. That undeserving partner has a choice: they can either radiate the same low vibration in which they suffered into the universe, or they can learn the lesson that the universe was teaching them and think about themselves before trying to be a "healer" for poorly matched partners.

It is a paradox of toxicity that can spiral out of control and affect many people's lives. I think we can all relate to toxic situations where we've been faced with choices. I have certainly acted in a way that has shown a toxic situation from the past has affected my decision-making. I've carried the experience of a toxic relationship into my own vibration upon entering a new relationship. This set a toxic precedent from the beginning of this new relationship—and the volatile atmosphere

I contributed to bred further toxicity. Many relationships break down due to this. Despite being compatible in interests, ambitions, and worldview, a certain "timing" of emotional baggage doesn't allow the relationship to thrive.

It is important to understand the past is the past, and you want to be the person who breaks that chain of toxicity. It ends with you. Also, it will not affect your friends, family, or coworkers in the future.

In my "Life After War" episode of *The Purpose Cycle Podcast*, I spoke to Shaun Docherty, an army veteran from the UK. Shaun admitted his *Purpose* is to become the best father he can possibly be, due to the lack of a father figure he experienced throughout childhood. "It wasn't about me anymore. I wanted to make her (his wife) proud." For some of us, the mesocycle (the longer-term *Purpose Cycle*) is achieving something internally for the benefit of others. Shaun's goals (microcycles) were centered around his work, but his broader *Purpose Cycle* (his mesocycle) was to build a happy and secure family.

He admits upon leaving the army, he wasn't in the correct frame of mind to achieve his *Purpose* and start a family. He had to truly find himself and the *Realizations* in those years became much clearer: "I didn't want to waste time with people who didn't want the same things as me." He also admitted he wanted to be the father he needed when he was younger, so he understood he could not care for others when he wasn't able to care for himself. Just like the airport analogy of applying your own oxygen mask before helping others apply theirs. If your heart is empty and unfulfilled, you cannot provide that fulfillment to others. Shaun followed the three steps of *Creation* in a slightly different manner:

- **Research**—he developed an understanding of what he wanted from his father and what he wanted to provide for his future children. He had the experience of role models and had the *Self-Realization* of what his inner child was missing in adulthood.
- **Strategize**—understanding he wasn't in a place to provide for a family, Shaun designed his life from living in a council flat in huge amounts of debt to forging a new career pathway, beginning as a truck driver to get familiar with the type of industry he would become a successful leader in. He told his wife, "In order to be successful, I'll have to take risks now before we have children."
- **Act**—Shaun meticulously chose the route which would get him financially secure. He took risks which led to owning properties and providing additional streams of income. All of these things would provide him with feelings of success and hits of oxytocin, serotonin, and endorphins. Ultimately it was the birth of his two sons and providing them with a stable and happy life that has given Shaun the *Fruition* of what he had worked so hard for and is a far cry from the soldier who left the army in his early twenties.

The situations that are provided to us quite often have underlying signals and messages for us to learn from. These can either inspire us or teach us. An event as tragic as losing a pet or a loved one teaches us about recovering from grief. It could show us how others deal with the same pain, so you know you need to be there for them during tough times. If you flip this scenario on its head, you see a positive situation can also build resilience, persevering through tough times, and coming out the other side to help other people. You see these situations happen to friends, family, or role models, and you may want that too. This could be something like purchasing a new home or getting a promotion at work. Once you begin to read situations and understand things happen *for* us, not *to* us, you will begin to prosper.

Reflecting on situations is always the best foot forward, as we often struggle to see the true message while engulfed in emotion. Hindsight is a wonderful thing, so use it to reframe your initial beliefs into something that will serve you. It is often a belief from lazy people that they should be winning after only doing a tiny amount of work. Going to the gym for a week doesn't mean you're in shape. Starting an Instagram doesn't earn you ten thousand followers right away. The true mindset of a champion is that you put in a huge amount of work and still worry about coming in second place. Adopt a similar mindset to contextualize that the amount of work you are putting in now will pay you back in the long-term. In the meantime, find nuggets of fulfillment to grant small rewards for the progress you're making, but don't ever be just satisfied with a little success when you have so much more that you can achieve.

CHAPTER 12

Tasks

TASK 9: YOUR WORTHY RIVAL

On a piece of paper, draw and label the characteristics of your worthy rival:

- What strengths do they have?
- What do you possess that they don't?
- What work are they doing that you are not?
- Final step for this exercise: I want you to **communicate** with them! Ask them about how they acquired certain strengths and see what you can learn from them.

TASK 10—DO SOMETHING NEW

For your next task, I am going to ask you to take on the fear of the unknown. I want you to fall in love with the process and understand you will gain joy from putting yourself through short-term hardship. You are going to spend the next seven days doing something that you may not necessarily want to do. You are going to try one small thing each day and build it up. Then I want you to choose one of these things you found the hardest to do (but probably got the most satisfaction when it was over) to do each day in your routine. This builds joy in discipline—and this makes your mindset bulletproof.

	My example	Your turn
Monday	Cold shower, wake up	
Tuesday	Cold shower, and drink four liters of water	
Wednesday	Cold shower, drink four liters of water, and eat vegetables with every meal	
Thursday	Cold shower, drink four liters of water, eat vegetables with every meal, and run to the gym	
Friday	Cold shower, drink four liters of water, eat vegetables with every meal, run to the gym, and fifty pushups upon waking up	
Saturday	Cold shower, drink four liters of water, eat vegetables with every meal, run to the gym, fifty pushups upon waking up, and phone switch-off	
Sunday	Cold shower, drink four liters of water, eat vegetables with every meal, run to the gym, fifty pushups upon waking up, phone switch-off, and run along the beach, Sea dip wake-up	
I am going to continue	Cold shower daily and aim to drink three to four liters of water daily.	

This helps you develop a range of choices you can use to challenge yourself. If I found myself slipping back to comfort, I could throw in another challenge I found hard. None of these challenges are overly tasking. They are small choices that are easy to say "no" to, but what they will do is provide you with that tiny piece of momentum that will begin a snowball of daily progression.

TESTING MOMENTS

As well as instant gratification, you will encounter other enemies to your success along the way. One of these is the safety zone your mind will want you to revert back to in times of struggle. We are limited when we are in our comfort zones, but when we push out of them, we become limitless.

I've previously mentioned motivation being like fuel, all vehicles eventually run out of fuel, and there will be times when it'll need refueling. Unlike a car, a plane, or a motorcycle, you will be able to operate without fuel—once you learn the art of discipline for internal rewards.

Remember: giving up is choosing the short-term you over the long-term you. If you go to the gym, you will be tired, and probably not much greater than before you started—but over time, the benefits compound, and that is where results appear. We all have bad days, but you know what the best thing about a bad day is? It ends at midnight. You can then wake up and go again.

LESSONS LEARNED FROM *CREATION*:

1. **There are three main stages to *Creation*: *Research, Strategize, Act.*** Plan your moves in silence, then shock them with results. Two additional elements to this are to *Reflect* and *Repeat.*

2. **To defeat the limiting beliefs, you must become a worthy rival.** Ask yourself what do your competitors have that you don't. Use this to look within and see what you need to improve on. Don't confuse this with trying to become someone else.

3. **Use IMPACT ideas to produce effective results in what you are trying to achieve.** It is a great way to break down your ideas when strategizing and reflecting.

Three lessons I've learned about myself from Creation *is:*

1.

2.

3.

Key Character trait: **Joy, love the process and love what you have become.**

PART 5

FRUITION

CHAPTER 13

Found

---

22 AND 23

The flight touched down back in Manchester, and it all became real: the version of myself on that couch in Spain almost a year ago was completely different from the one who embarked on his mission to become a business owner. I had done the research of what it took to design a successful coaching business, I had strategized meticulously how I was going to execute this plan, and I could finally act. I had made calls and emails prior to catching my flight home, and I had my first clients lined up and ready.

As a young man, one of the main pitfalls I saw in myself, and others, is pride and ego. Dr. Rick Rigsby gives an amazing quote in his book *Lessons from a Third Grade Dropout*: "Pride is the burden of a foolish person." I was fortunate enough with my upbringing to understand nothing was "beneath me." I have previously mentioned ego not consuming your choices, and I needed cash if I was to make this business a success. Therefore, within a week of returning back to the UK working on my *Fruition*, I was back working in the coffee shop I had previously worked in before my flight out to the states. The only difference this time being I finally had direction.

I had *Purpose*.

Understanding a proposed "stop-gap" situation is fine. As long as it doesn't snowball into a dead-end job. The management knew of my ambitions and were kind enough to place me in morning shifts so I could fill my afternoons with coaching work. This way, I could maintain an income while pursuing my dreams, and the income I was getting from my sports coaching was a small taste of the life I was creating. I was offered work in a variety of schools, even my boyhood football club. I was hugely honored to be recognized for the value of what I was doing, and it started to become apparent what you do in the *Creation* phase comes to bear fruit if you remain consistent and effective over time.

Gradually, the shifts in the coffee shop became less frequent. I will always be so grateful for the lessons in teamwork, communication, and hard work that being employed there taught me. I often ponder "what would have been" if I had remained in my comfort zone because it was a job I loved but just didn't align with my *Purpose*.

My *Purpose* was to inspire the next generation to take up football, learn new skills, and develop their own ambitions for success. I loved every minute of it. There was lots of driving around, being alone, and not many guaranteed hours, but each time I stepped onto the field, I brought enthusiasm, passion, and quality to everything I taught. So much so the hours became more and more frequent. I was attracting more success and more opportunities. My new environment dictated my results, and I created one I could thrive in.

When I quoted Matthew McConaughey in my *Initiation* section, I asked you to chase your hero. Now in the *Fruition* stage, I needed to realign my criteria for my new hero. I could feel the person who was so lost at the beginning now found. The acceptance I thought I needed from my peers for all of those years was gone. The only acceptance I needed was from myself—and I finally had that.

For the next twelve months, I worked meticulously on plans to launch my business. I was now twenty-three, a new *Aspiration* had emerged: I wanted to become an incredibly successful business owner. I saw the life my superiors lived in the states. I saw the life the DeLeeuw family had built for themselves. For this first *Purpose Cycle*, I worked on myself to destroy childhood limiting beliefs and understand my place in the world. The *Fruition* felt *amazing*, and it sparked the desire to succeed more.

The business was building well for myself. Although I was growing, I found it hard to scale the business on my own. I needed an investment; I needed an opportunity to become "The Boss." not just "my own boss." This is where the twenty-three timeline begins. I first saw the advert to propose my business idea to a board of already successful business owners.

What dawned on me from my first *Purpose Cycle* is conforming to the social desires of others led to a low-challenge life. During my time at university, I identified the characteristics of my former self as a procrastinator, anxious, over-thinker.

I left as a positive-minded, self-development enthusiast who was aware of his faults and ready to work on them. The one trait I always had was ambition, but ambition is nothing without the desire to work without instant results. I discovered everything is learned, and the path you walk in life isn't already determined for you. There is always time to start.

26

After three years, I went from a disillusioned twenty-something to now being a student teacher. This was by far the toughest cycle of all. I had to learn how to cope with the grief of losing one of my best friends in the process of rediscovering my *Purpose*. A quote from my friend Stephen that his parents had discovered on his phone shortly after he passed away had stuck with all of his friends: "If you're not making someone else's life better, then you're wasting your time."

I had used this quote somewhat as a motto on how I was going to live my life, and I reflected on what I was really doing: turning up for an hour a day at a different location. Yes, these children were enjoying the sessions I was delivering but was I really having an impact on their lives? Was I truly inspiring them to discover their dreams and begin to manifest them? To have a true impact, I felt like I had to become a permanent feature in one place. Where everybody would actually know my name and I could build a rapport with the staff and pupils rather than bounce around from place to place. Funnily enough, that's when the call came.

"Jon, we've loved the work you have been doing here, and I wanted to offer you a place for an interview on a teacher training course. Did you want to attend the interview?"

This was it! I was bearing fruit from the consistency of showing up and giving my all into the various sessions. I thought back to Dan's question all those years ago: "What is important to you?" Well, *this*! A permanent place of work where I could be the constant source of inspiration to the young minds is important to me. This was what I wanted, and it all aligned with my *Purpose*.

As you can probably imagine, the parting of ways wasn't particularly amicable. Closing down the coaching company in profit was seen as a success by myself—due to the fact most start-up companies fail within the first year—but to him, not so much.

"You're going to regret this," said Dan.

"Yep, thanks for the opportunity. I believe this is the path I should take."

A short period of awkwardness when I was refused an amicable handshake, and I was free! My new *Aspiration* phase was just starting, and I was still feeling the benefits of *Fruition*. The money I had earned during my time with the business paid for my university course to become a teacher. I was also free of the negativity, and that was a huge emotional weight that had been lifted. Bumping into some of the staff who had worked for my former business partner proved I had made the correct choice. They told me he was telling everyone he had fired me. The greatest thing about the *Fruition* phase is you are so happy you feel bulletproof against negativity. So, I just smiled, had a little laugh to myself, and wished them all a nice day. To be at peace with yourself is true *Fruition*. The feeling that nothing can deter you from acting in line with your new identity.

Walking into my new school as a new man was a fantastic feeling. I had reinvented myself from previous cycles. This is what we do as humans. We level up! Each cycle, we upgrade ourselves and become a better version than before. I entered the building confident, excited, and ready to take on any challenge and meet like-minded mentors with whom I shared a similar *Purpose*.

This was when I met Mike, my first role model in the education sector: "Nice to meet you, Jon. I've heard a lot about you, and I can't wait to begin working with you and helping our children."

This was it. The moment where twenty-six began and a new *Purpose Cycle* was born. *Fruition* breeds new *Aspirations*. The danger of aiming so relentlessly for a goal is once that goal is achieved and the pot of gold is reached, many people don't have a plan. They ask themselves, "What next?" when it is too late. Instead, always ask yourself, "What next?" so new *Aspirations* can emerge after your *Fruition*.

30

I often wondered where Mike was in his career since leaving shortly after my third *Purpose Cycle* started and I became a teacher. During the short time, he was present during my *Aspiration* stage. His influence stuck with me throughout. He helped bring out the spark that was inside me all along, but other role models helped nurture that flame along the way.

Having gained four years of experience in the teaching world, I had a clearer picture of what the *Aspiration* was in my twenty-six timeline. I wanted to inspire professionals to reach their potential while still having a greater impact on shaping young people's lives for the better. When you manifest a dream with enough conviction and certitude, your timeline could throw opportunities at you to prepare you for the ultimate *Fruition*.

This is the case because the universe understands you're heading in the right direction, but you need something extra to help shape you into your future you. After all, you can't do everything on your own. The energy you put out to your environment will dictate the path in which you want to go on, but the environment (or universe) will ultimately decide what is right for you at that moment in time. Think back to Bob Proctor's quote on the Law of Vibration: "We literally live in an ocean of motion."

Another day had finished, and I was organizing my work for the next day when an email came up with a job advertisement in the school where I taught. It was the role Mike had held when I first began my teaching career. What I had done in my day-to-day *Creation* led to this. I felt compelled to apply. I was only four years into my career, but as I mentioned in the paragraph above, I believe the universe decided to send this opportunity my way.

My first *Purpose Cycle* was about finding my place in the world, my second timeline was about finding my values, and my third led me to finding my future.

A successful application led to an interview. I knew for a fact I was not the front-runner to take on the role. How could I be? My experience was not as much as the other candidates. You can manifest all you want, but when the situation comes down to the present moment—a sense of realism needs to be applied. We could all manifest to "make our first million tomorrow," but it won't happen unless you work toward your goal over a sustained period of time. I followed the steps to *Creation*: researching other role models in leadership positions which I wanted, strategizing what I needed to learn and improving in those areas to get there, and acting on those two previous steps. Walking into the interview, I knew I couldn't have done more to act on those building blocks. It was all down to what was right for me at this point in my journey.

I came out of my interview with an overwhelming feeling of positive energy. I knew even if I was not successful, I gave it my best shot and didn't leave anything out there. Understanding the steps of the *Purpose Cycle* and contextualizing life's seasons brings positive energy to your actions. Nothing is left to luck, and you are performing at your optimum. I had never delivered a presentation like it. I answered the questions well, and a wash of acceptance over-roared me. Then came the call back to the meeting room. Was it my turn to become the new "Mark?"

The news wasn't what I wanted to hear, but I needed to hear it.

The job wasn't mine.

Strangely, I didn't feel an ounce of disappointment. I spoke about worthy rivals earlier in the book, and this is exactly why they *have* to be present in your *Purpose Cycle*. Without an element of competition, it is much more difficult to engage high-performing employees. The feeling of acceptance was not one of "giving up." It was an understanding that the universe had thrown this opportunity in to show my bosses my intentions to progress, and although I wasn't ready *yet*, I knew I would be one day. Just because I didn't have the same job title as Mike didn't mean I couldn't inspire and lead just like he did. Your *Purpose* isn't binary; it isn't dictated by the label of a job title, age, or experience.

The timeline brought forward an opportunity that I aspired to gain a couple of years from now. So, the whole process of applying for the same job my first mentor in education had is one I thank the universe for and show my gratitude to my environment for allowing me to go through that particular process. It gave me the taste of *Fruition* I needed to keep going.

If you're interpreting this final timeline as "Not all stories have happy endings," then let me correct that thought: They do. Every story *you* take charge of has a happy ending. A quote attributed to John Lennon springs to mind: "Everything will be okay in the end. If it's not okay, it's not the end" (Zeal, 2017).

Not every stage of *Fruition* is the result you were expecting or, in my case, hoping for. What you must do is process that event with the same poise as you would a victory. For many, they may see failing in a job interview as something that will crush them. The question you must ask is this: Have you learned more about yourself from going through this experience? Heck, I spent my early twenties applying for jobs I didn't want just so I could improve at public speaking and being interviewed for jobs. By the time I went for a job I really wanted, I felt comfortable in that situation. Become comfortable with the uncomfortable, and you will feel an immense feeling of satisfaction afterward.

Upon arriving back home, I felt elation, joy, and calmness. Having that sense of clarity about where your life is going brings these feelings. Bumps in the road are merely stepping-stones to success. There is no sense of disgruntlement, bitterness, or even sadness. The best person for the role got the job. Life works in that way, and you can see from the other candidates' *Creations* how their *Fruition* evolved. I know my day will come.

A new *Aspiration*—similar to my twenty-six timeline of wanting to become a leader—has ignited. A wonderful aspect of the *Purpose Cycle* is every situation you face is interpreted in a positive manner to act as a building block to the ultimate you. Challenges along the way are welcomed. I have developed over the years a fantastic relationship with failure. From someone who would artificially create climates where I couldn't lose (remaining in the comfort zone), I am now somebody who throws myself into the deep end and the unknown. I welcome it.

I often think back to the challenges of the previous two *Purpose Cycles* to see how it has helped me deal with challenges I either presently face or may face in the future. Life can whiz past us in a flash sometimes. We often focus so much on climbing the mountain and looking at how far we have to go we forget to look back on how far we've come.

In the *Creation* phase, I became the living embodiment of my dream-self. I became the leader I had aspired to be. Just because I had yet to receive the rank of "leader" didn't mean I couldn't lead by example. My *Purpose* had expanded. I didn't want to just inspire the thirty minds of the children I was working with. I wanted to inspire young people on a broader scale. This is where I was given the platform to deliver impact to every single child within that setting. My boss also gave me the platform to deliver impact to fellow professionals and student teachers.

The feeling this brings is incredible. The day-to-day fulfillment of *Purpose* feels greater every single time you reach the *Fruition* stage on a new cycle because you've worked so hard, faced so much adversity, and overcome many challenges and doubters that the satisfaction is compounded through the other cycles. This allows you to dream bigger, and that is exactly what I have done to this day.

Reflecting during a time of crisis across the world with the COVID-19 pandemic, I was feeling a great sense of contentment toward the goals I had achieved. I could see the impact my work was having on others, and I was being internally rewarded by this with bouts of *Fruition*. However, upon writing a speech for my students, it became apparent a new

Aspiration was emerging: I wanted to inspire people on a global scale by writing this book.

CHAPTER 14

Fulfillment

Success breeds dreams, and in every experience I had through the timelines, I found the light in the darkest times. I also used momentum as a huge catalyst for further development. This is why we started in the *Aspiration* stage by changing the way we talked and our self-perception. Rounding all aspects of our life (such as finances, health, education, and career) is a difficult task, and in my research for this book, I came across a concept that aligned with my message so profoundly.

The Japanese concept of *Ikigai* has no direct English translation—but it basically means "the embodiment of happiness in living." Having discovered this concept very late in the research of this book, it could've been quite easy to discard it as another synonym for "purpose" or "direction." But when you understand the term dating back to the Heian period of 794 AD (and more recently by Akihiro Hasegawa), it becomes evident finding *Purpose* in life is a critical part of living—and shouldn't be overlooked (Garcia, 2017).

Fig. 4—A model of Ikigai

The reason why you get up in the morning is Ikigai, the reason why you bought this book is Ikigai, and the reason you're going to be a better person year after year is—you guessed it—Ikigai! This concept essentially links a multitude of facets in your life and contextualizes them—very similar to the *Purpose Cycle*. However, the *Purpose Cycle* certainly hones in on the top to inner areas of "Passion" and "Mission" and tries to apply it to "Profession" and "Vocation." Ultimately, you are discovering yourself, as cliché as it may sound, and finding a perfect harmony of different areas in your life brings *Purpose*, or "Ikigai."

However, for some Japanese people, the idea is slightly different. They believe *Purpose* may have nothing to do with income. In fact, according to a 2017 BBC Worklife article, a survey of two thousand Japanese men and women was conducted by Central Research Services in 2010 and found only 31 percent of recipients considered work as their Ikigai. They found a greater *Purpose* in life than their work. They sought family as the main strand of their *Purpose*. This isn't contrary to what I have stated during this entire journey, but what we could argue is if these people truly looked at their professions and vocations, they would play a larger part in their *Purpose* by either financially giving them the tools to act on *Purpose*, or having a greater, direct impact on their *Purpose*.

Regardless, the *Purpose Cycle* and Ikigai link very closely. Both models contextualize areas within your life you have control over and can influence to feel "complete," which is, as we've discovered in this book, the *Fruition* stage.

Being complete is the feeling of satisfaction when you progress through the levels. It is the sense of accomplishment at the end of the task. You don't have to feel complete at the end of your journey in life, nor should you feel guilty for wanting more. Finding meaning in your life by understanding what your passion is and how it can provide substance to the world is one of the fascinating aspects of life. We often compare ourselves to others, but we are ignorant to the fact we all offer something different to the world. What makes *you* unique is you have something to offer the world, and you are reading this book to better yourself.

The two ingredients to success, *Purpose*, and meaning are a passionate "why" and a willingness to work hard and give your "why" substance. According to Garcia, in *Ikigai*, "To those in Japan who follow Ikigai, they believe that the small joys in everyday life result in a feeling of fulfillment," therefore, long-term *Fruition*. We shouldn't view happiness as a destination: more so a state of mind we can regularly access.

Even in times when we feel really low, understand those feelings are temporary—and we can regularly access the nuggets of fulfillment when we stop for a moment and look around. Look at the home you have worked hard toward, look at the joy on your children's faces, look at your partner/spouse. What more do you actually need? If basic needs are met like food, water, shelter (thinking back to Maslow), then everything else is an opportunity to be greater, live more versatile, and use those nuggets of happiness to outweigh the difficult times. Relating it back to the mountain analogy at the beginning of the book, we often focus on how much of the mountain we are yet to climb, we often forget to look back on how far we've come.

Just like you, I am constantly exploring myself, pushing boundaries, and trying new things. Ten years ago, writing this book would've seemed like a pipe dream! During your journey reading this book, you have looked inward and explored yourself. The question is: What is your *Purpose*? Can you relate to struggles, challenges, or successes I have had along the way? How many *Purpose Cycles* have you experienced in your life? *The Purpose Cycle* is thought-provoking. It encourages you to consciously think about the direction you are heading. While writing this book, I identified with the many different stages. It is hard to follow your own advice at times, but once you develop your self-awareness to the point in which you are comfortable with acknowledging shortfalls or understand you need to truly discover your passion, then you are already heading in a positive direction.

Intertwined within each phase is a theme of compassion. Although it may not be explicit in each phase, you must act with compassion as an overseeing characteristic throughout this process of self-improvement. We cannot advance as people without it, and it allows us to improve others around us as well as ourselves. Whenever you get the opportunity to be a "good person," take it. How do you feel afterward? Because your values are lodged internally, then the small things such as: holding a door open for a person, encouraging others around you to succeed, or giving a hug to that person who needs a 'pick me up' all compound fulfillment to make you feel incredible! If you exude that aura, then you will continue to attract greater opportunities. To live a positive life, you must live in a positive mindset.

The simple message about *Fruition* is you've visualized what it was you wanted; you've understood what you need to change to get there. You've made the first steps in being the "new you"; you've remained consistent and disciplined while overcoming the challenges along the way, and now you can look back at how successful you have been on that journey.

Now that you understand the *Purpose Cycle*, I envisage your goals stepping up a level, as should our *Aspirations* each time. The likelihood is most of you started with a small change—a job promotion, a health goal—and now it's time to dream big. What does your macrocycle look like? What microcycles do you need to accomplish along the way? Advancing your goals is parallel with a video game. The greater the vision, the greater the challenges you'll face. As my father once told me, "A winner never quits, and quitters never win," which still resonates with me to this day.

DEVELOPING EMOTIONAL INTELLIGENCE

During this whole process, you will have learned a great deal about yourself. *Fruition* is not only about reaping the positive outcomes from your *Purpose Cycle* but also about understanding the lessons you have learned during your growth. Many different situations arise during personal journeys, and all of these contribute to building up resilience and, most importantly, your emotional intelligence.

Emotional intelligence, by definition, is one's ability to recognize, be aware of, and in control of their own emotional reactions and those of others. The concept of emotional intelligence was first created back in 1995 by Daniel Goleman. In his book, quite fittingly called *Emotional intelligence*, Goleman talks about how an emotionally intelligent person is able to differentiate between his emotions and is able to use them to navigate their thoughts and actions. Though this is easier said than done, there are certain guidelines to follow if you want to take control over your emotions and reactions.

THE 5 ABILITIES TO HELP YOU TAKE CONTROL

To take control over your emotions and reactions and keep them regulated (instead of having them control you), there are five main abilities to focus on and develop (Goleman, 2012):

1. Empathy

At its very core, empathy is one's ability to put themselves in other people's shoes and understand their thought patterns, emotions, reactions, feelings, and behaviors.

In doing so, you will realize there is no ultimate truth!

Everyone is bound to their own belief system and their own encoded emotional responses and thought patterns. It is our role as caring human beings to be able to understand that perspective and at the very least acknowledge why a person is feeling a particular way. After all, I talk in my blog on thepurposecycle.com about how five people will give varied accounts of the same situation, despite them all witnessing the same thing.

2. Self-Awareness

This second ability can manifest on many different levels, but when it comes to emotional intelligence, it is, in fact, crucial. Being able to recognize your own emotions, feelings, thoughts, behaviors, and reactions is of prime importance when you are becoming more emotionally intelligent. Though recognizing them is important, it is just half the battle. The other half is to actually make conscious choices and break those patterns. We all learn from experience, so don't ever blame yourself for undergoing certain emotions. Only blame yourself if you don't learn from them.

3. Discipline

In the modern world, it is believed there is a "once and for all" solution to all your emotional problems/depression. Well, the truth is there is no such thing as permanent happiness because, as humans, we constantly surf the entire emotional spectrum as long as we are alive! That is why new *Aspirations* are born from a person's *Fruition*. Staying consistent and disciplined with physical and emotional well-being practices is important when you are building your emotional intelligence. The more you can maintain when you're not at your optimum means you'll reap more when the time comes to win.

The fact of the matter is you will not always be 100 percent motivated toward your goals, but it doesn't mean you don't want to be successful anymore. That is why putting in place routines and systems that allow dips in motivation on your road to success.

4. Self-Regulation

At its very core, self-regulation is an important ability to develop, which is at the very core of emotional intelligence. This is one's ability to control their emotions and actions leading after the emotions. Even if you lose it and fall for the automatic reactions encoded into you, well-developed self-regulation will mean you'll recover much quicker after an emotional reaction. To become stronger in this area, you must be able to detach yourself emotionally from a situation to become your own counsel. "How would I advise somebody else to react in this situation?" should be a question at the forefront of any *Realizations* you may be having.

5. Social Intelligence

As emotional humans, we must realize our emotional states affect others, especially when they are in our environment. Social emotional intelligence is one's ability to control their emotions and reactions in a social environment.

Does emotional intelligence equal happiness?

As we already mentioned, there is this global idea that there are certain actions you can take, which will result in eternal, life-long happiness, with the absence of bad emotions. However, this is simply not true! Even more so, as social beings, we are all different, and we all have a set of emotional responses and reactions. The differences between people are a premise for problems and conflicts, but if emotional intelligence is present on at least one side, there would be a certain level of understanding, which can alleviate any personal or social conflict. On top of that, emotional intelligence allows us to be more aware of what we feel under certain circumstances. This, therefore, gives us a greater level of adaptability, which in turn helps us make the right choices in the more important aspects of life.

For the most part, humans have a specific set of encoded emotional responses and reactions, which, for the most part, are automatic. These behaviors belong to a part of our nervous system called the "limbic brain" (Lautin, 2007). This is the part of the brain that holds the emotional fight or flight responses. You didn't really choose to be that way; those things were literally given to you when you were a child. They were given to you by your parents, siblings, other relatives, teachers, friends, etc. The beauty of it is this changes as you mature and get wiser. After all, they say you are the average of the five people you are closest to.

Emotional intelligence is about recognizing those automatic responses and asking yourself, "Who gave me that, and do I really need it to affect me that way?" After setting that *Self-Realization*, your next step is to take conscious action and take control over your emotions instead of letting them control you. This is what *Fruition* truly is: becoming completely self-aware and at peace with yourself. Even if you're not where you want to get to long-term, you are at peace with the fact you are heading toward ultimate *Fruition*.

CHAPTER 15

Tasks

In the next task, you will revisit your manifestation exercise from the beginning of the book and understand how you have developed in each of those five areas to inevitably develop your emotional intelligence.

TASK 11—BACK AT THE MOVIES

We completed this exercise back in the *Aspiration* section of the book. You may have revisited this exercise, but don't worry if not. It is an amazing way to compare.

Picture yourself in a cinema, surrounded by people who have been with you and supporting you during this journey. The countdown starts in that old-fashioned cinema style from ten down to zero. The anticipation builds; the excitement is burning within you. You have unlocked the secret to your success— and your closest circle are here to witness it.

The film comes on and it is you. The film is a Purpose Cycle. *It could be multiple microcycles, it could be a mesocycle (medium-term), but the long-term macrocycle is not shown...*

You are being your dream-self, overcoming all of the challenges you have faced along the way. Like every good storyline, there have been times where you've been tested, but these never lasted forever. You got back up again and acted in accordance with your dream-self. Your small wins turn into opportunities, which in turn prospers into large victories, which lead to where you are now—Fruition. There could be notable people missing from the cinema. This is fine. You are at peace with yourself, and you're so fixated on the film that you know those who mean the most to you are by your side.

This film never cuts back to the past because the old film burned up, remember? The new film represents you. You were the director, and you brought your own Fruition. You are feeling daily fulfillment and want to continue into another Purpose Cycle.

This is where the film leaves on an incredible teasing note. The audience around you wanted to see more. You know there must be a sequel to this. Repeat the exercise over time to visualize that sequel. What does future Fruition look like? Can you believe how wonderful you feel as you picture it?

My calling to write this book was because there were people who were "sleepwalking" through life. I have a fear of reflecting at the age of seventy-five, thinking, "I wish I had done X," or, "I missed an opportunity to do Y." That same fear also overcame me when I dealt with other people.

I saw this was more evident than ever during the COVID-19 pandemic. The entire world stopped still; people stood still. A compelling feeling came over me to extend my *Aspiration* to inspire young people; it became to inspire people, period. What surprised me was how the idea of *The Purpose Cycle* came about. Writing a five-minute speech for my class turned into sharing my idea globally. It's a journey I have loved, and I am well aware this is igniting a brand-new *Aspiration* internally.

My view of the world has opened up tremendously, and what I am grateful for the most is being able to speak with so many people in the making of this book. A true social network was established more so than one where communicating via a double-tap was the medium of approval. True conversation flowed, and I have learned a great deal from people's life experiences. Everyone has a book in them. Within mine, I wanted to inspire you to metaphorically become the director of your own life, the writer of your own book, and the artist of your own painting. Too many people let societal norms make huge life decisions for us, mostly down to one of the four fears. Now you understand the concept of *Realization*. You're able to look at a situation objectively and make a positive step forward.

It could be argued the term cycle implies there is a continual path that has no perceived end goal. Announcing to yourself you have "made it" can be quite a dangerous prospect; is there ever a true end to a pursuit of fulfillment? Once you have the car, you want the house. Once you have the house, you want a bigger house, and so on. Fulfillment isn't a tangible place nor a destination. It is merely a state of mind. If you can have nuggets of fulfillment without feeling fulfilled...

I called this *Fruition* because you are reaping the rewards of past groundwork without feeling like the journey is complete. This is not necessarily a negative trait to have; settling can be perceived as complacency. Set a relentless pursuit in a positive, abundant manner and say, "I have done this, now to build on this and move on to the next level," rather than, "Although I have done this, I wish I had more." This dangerous, scarcity approach will only lead to one thing: being negativity enrolled in a *Purpose Cycle*. We continue to frame our life through the lens of a high-challenge/ high-success life, not a low-challenge life.

Each cycle you design needs to be approached with a positive, growth-orientated state of mind. There will come a point in time in your life when you will have undergone several *Purpose Cycles* and eventually "made it" at fulfillment. That is when you can sit back, relax, and reminisce on all of the ups and downs, ebbs and flows of your journey—but today is *not* that day.

You've just discovered this concept—so where to next? Another *Purpose Cycle* for sure, but how exactly do you "level up?" Only you can answer that question as a new *Aspiration* finds you. Searching for it is not necessarily a bad thing, but more often than not, an *Aspiration* will jump out at you. You could be washing the dishes, tucking yourself into bed, running around the neighborhood, or just walking the dog when a new idea hits you. Then it's time to begin another life-changing *Purpose Cycle*.

The great thing about this concept is that it is completely subjective to everyone. For somebody, success will be becoming a manager of the bar they work in. For others, it will be obtaining their degree, and others obtaining their driver's license. You may be reading this book and successfully starting a side-hustle that's quickly shaping into a successful full-time business, or you could be reaching your initial fitness goals with the purpose of entering a competition. What I'm basically getting at is no matter your *Aspiration*, protect it, consider it, and pursue it. You never know how far you may take it.

LESSONS LEARNED FROM *FRUITION*:

1. ***Fruition* is not the end; it is merely the beginning.** You will undergo many *Purpose Cycles* in your life, and the wonderful thing about the *Purpose Cycle* is you have seen in my timelines I continuously reinvent myself throughout the stories.

2. ***Fruition* is completely internal.** There are many factors that can offer you nuggets of fulfillment, but the true feeling of happiness and *Fruition* comes from the feeling of Ikigai—your life aligning in many different ways, which, in turn, provides you with more.

3. **Being a compassionate person is the ultimate *Fruition*.** By developing your emotional intelligence, you will gravitate to incredible opportunities, people, and experiences so long as you practice gratitude and act in a compassionate manner toward yourself and others. That is the true secret to success.

Three lessons I've learned about myself from **Fruition** *is:*

1.

2.

3.

Key Character trait: **Compassion**

Conclusion

To deliver a message to as many people as possible became the goal. The message is it is never "too late" to realize and manifest your dream life. I found myself in a state of disillusion at various points in my life. In each of these timelines, I began to contextualize what it was that I was experiencing. These feelings were never forever; they could be short-, medium-, or longer-term, but they were never eternal. That is when the idea came to me: *The Purpose Cycle*.

As soon as I reached each goal in these stories, a new *Aspiration* began. I was ready for the next journey, better equipped than the last. The starting point almost felt like a staircase. I wasn't starting from the bottom step each time. I was starting from a higher point and a better foundation. Discovering *Purpose* is holistic to what we do with our lives, but the ways of achieving said *Purpose* can develop and grow stronger over time.

From being a young student who wasn't even able to inspire himself to having found my *Purpose* and having now written a book that is accessible worldwide, it is almost impossible to see the end goal, only the next goal. Because what you think is the ultimate end goal is merely the beginning of a new *Aspiration*, that very thought is what excites me to drive forward each day.

Now isn't the time to give up, nor is it to rest on your laurels. Don't pause to measure your riches, to see how much you have. Don't count your awards and seek more. Don't be greedy. When things are going well, let the winnings come and be grateful, but don't pay too much attention to the numbers on the bank statement or the number of followers you have.

Fruition is the time to give yourself inner credit for what you've shown: resilience in the face of adversity, attention to detail in the *Creation* phase, genius when plotting a new idea. Enjoy the *Fruition*, and there'll be plenty of time for the feeling of fulfillment later in life. Find pathways and *Purpose Cycles* that are less strenuous, like building a garden or decorating a room for the grandchildren.

Only then should you look outwardly and take stock of your achievements, praise, accolades, and financial *Fruition*. This will be your "rocking chair" moment, as I call it, where you will sit reminiscing about all you have achieved.

My biggest fear was (and still is in many ways) that "rocking chair" moment and feeling regret. I always believed in making a million mistakes rather than making up a million excuses why I can't do it. Every single day a new grain of sand drops in the sand timer—the finite element of life is what makes us seize the day. None of us know how long we truly have left, so don't count the days, make the days count! After all, the one currency you spend daily without any control is *time*. What you can control is *how* you spend that time. Many of us realize this when it appears to be too late, but if you're not sitting reading this in your rocking chair, then go and chase that *Aspiration*! Once you begin the *Purpose Cycle*, you will understand something (here is the "Fight Club" bombshell moment):

Every single phase of *The Purpose Cycle* is ever-present throughout our lives.

You may resonate closer with one phase stronger than another when going through a particular time, but you will constantly gain new *Aspiration*s. Your *Realizations* are ever emerging as you are always on a journey of self-discovery. You will encounter new beginnings with the *Initiation* phase and start again (never from scratch, as you always have a platform of experience to build from). You will be creating your dream life daily by researching new opportunities, strategizing your next moves, acting upon them, and finally bearing the fruits of what you have created for yourself.

Life is one huge *Purpose Cycle* paradox, which is essentially one macrocycle with many microcycles and mesocycles along the way. The beauty is that the cycles intertwine, and, in reality, we are all experiencing every stage each day—even if our stage of *Fruition* has nothing tangible to show for.

Next time, what will you do in the *Creation* stage to change this? *Fruition* is about knowing yourself truthfully and being self-aware enough to feel ready to take the next step in life. To be truly at peace with yourself is a form of *Infinite Fruition*—a complete *Purpose Cycle*. If I have one final message in this book, it is to remember you are defined by what you say, judged by what you do, and respected by how you treat others. Bring about positive changes to the life of others and notice your life take the same turn.

Acknowledgments

——

A special thank you to every single person mentioned in this book, regardless of context, for being a part of my life and for teaching me something valuable. Thank you to my close friends and my family. Many are not mentioned by name in my stories, but all of you have played a huge part in my life. I would also like to thank the following people for being a huge influence for writing this book but also shaping who I am today:

My amazing wife, Sarah Tucker. My family: Sam Tucker, David, and Tina Tucker. The Newlove Family, the Holmes Family, and my closest friends: Alex Wood, Rob Cheeseman, Liam Holiday, Scott Annandale, Anthony Verity, and Adam Douglas. Of course, my work family—the entire staff at Spring Cottage Primary School.

I'd like to thank the following families for changing my life in the nine months I spent in the United States of America. I will never forget the hospitality you gave me, and I hope to return to see you one day:

The Hollenback Family, the DeLeeuw Family, the Morris Family, the Kincaid Family, and the Goff Family.

I would also like to gratefully show my appreciation to these people who supported my presale campaign and turned this book from a Google Doc pipe dream into a tangible reality:

Sarah Tucker, Joe Todd, Liam Holiday, Shaun Docherty, Carl Lowery, Tim Holmes, Jane Holmes, Samantha Holmes, Connie Holmes, Emily Pawson, Susanne Varley, Hollie Godson, Oliver Coupland, Kenneth Newlove, Sarah K Newlove, Alex Wood, Sarah Middleton-Wood, Mia Coates, Owen Harrison, Charlotte Keelan, Sarah Hamilton, Hannah Polson, Adele Graham, Chelsey White, Maureen Varley, William Hollenback, Laura Rand, Melissa Francis, Sarah Spence, Sam Tucker, Lewis Walkington, Tina Tucker, Anthony Thomas Skoyles, Scott Annandale, Candice DeLeeuw, James Newlove, Richard Newlove, Katharine Hutty, Sherrie Reading, Sean Scott, Matt Scarr, Andrew Annandale, Jordan Reading, David Reading, Louisa Newlove, Mark Prendergast, David Tucker, Benn Broadhead, Rob Cheeseman, Sophie Godson, Benjamin Ian Verburg, Anthony Verity, Brian Gibson, Julie Verity, Rachael Dean, Phil Brown, Alex Newlove, Sarah Campbell, Alex Douglas, Bradley Wright, Sergey Kochergan, and Nigel Gan.

I'd like to extend my gratitude to my publisher, New Degree Press, for accepting my idea and bringing it to *Fruition* (pun intended!). Especially thank you to Professor Koester of the Creator Institute, who enabled my idea to grow. Thank you to my editors, Paloma Wristley and Sarah Lobrot, who have challenged me to make this idea the best it can be on paper.

Without the feedback and accountability check-ins, this book wouldn't have been possible. Finally, I want to thank the layout team, the images and cover designer team, the copy editors, as well as anyone who offered marketing advice during the campaign. The coolest moment of the experience for me was definitely hearing from my "self-help hero" Simon Sinek when he spoke at our Creator Institute meeting.

Lastly, I'd like to acknowledge a few sources of inspiration:

Ant Middleton, Rudyard Kipling, Ricky Gervais, Tom Bileyu, Jake Humphrey, True Geordie, Laurence McKenna, Neil Strauss, and the movie: *The Pursuit of Happyness.*

Finally, I would like to dedicate the final quote and acknowledgment to a friend who I miss every single day:

"If you're not making somebody else's life better, then you're wasting your time."

—STEPHEN HUGHES

You truly did live *One Amazing Life.*

Appendix

INTRODUCTION: WHAT IS *PURPOSE*

Dillard, Annie. *The Writing Life*. New York: Harper & Row, 1989.

Dunning, David, Kerri Johnson, Joyce Ehrlinger, and Justin Kruger. "Why People Fail to Recognize Their Own Incompetence." *Current Directions in Psychological Science 12*, no.3 (2003): 83–87.

Evans, Eleanor. "Personal Well-Being in the UK—Office for National Statistics." *Ons.Gov.Uk 2021*. https://www.ons.gov.uk/peoplepopulationandcommunity/wellbeing/bulletins/measuringnationalwellbeing/2015to2016.

King, Vex. *Good Vibes, Good Life (Gift Edition)*. London: Hay House UK Ltd, 2020.

CHAPTER 1

Clear, James. *Atomic Habits: Tiny Changes, Remarkable Results: An Easy & Proven Way to Build Good Habits & Break Bad Ones*. New York: Penguin Random House, 2018.

King, Vex. *Good Vibes, Good Life.* Gift Edition. London: Hay House UK Ltd, 2020.

Maslow, A.H. "A Theory of Human Motivation." *Psychological Review* 50, no. 4 (1943): 430–437.

Sinek, Simon. *Start with Why: How Great Leaders Inspire Everyone to Take Action.* Harlow, England: Penguin Books, 2011.

Woodward, Clive. "Great Teams Are Made up of Great Individuals." Nov 16, 2020. In *High Performance.* Produced by J. Humphrey, and D. Hughes. Podcast. https://www.thehighperformancepodcast.com/episodes/clive-woodward.

CHAPTER 2

Keng, Shao-Hsun, Chun-Hung Lin, and Peter F. Orazem. "Expanding College Access in Taiwan, 1978–2014: Effects on Graduate Quality and Income Inequality." *Journal of Human Capital* 11, no. 1 (Spring 2017): 9–10. https://doi.org/10.1086/690235.

Kilner, J M, and R N Lemon. "What We Know Currently about Mirror Neurons." *Current Biology* 23, (2013): 1057–62. https://doi.org/10.1016/j.cub.2013.10.051.

King, Vex. *Good Vibes, Good Life.* Gift Edition. London: Hay House UK Ltd, 2020.

Oxford English Dictionary. 2nd ed. s.v. "self-love." Accessed September 30, 2020. https://www.oxfordlearnersdictionaries.com/definition/english/self-love.

Prelec, Drazen, and Ronit Bodner. "*Self-Signaling and Self-Control.*" In *Time and decision: Economic and psychological perspectives on intertemporal choice,* edited by G. Loewenstein, D. Read, and R. Baumeister, 277–298. Russell Sage Foundation, 2003.

Starostinetskaya, Anna. "Veganuary Reports 85 Percent Success Rate." *Vegnews.Com.* Accessed August 15, 2021. https://vegnews.com/2021/4/veganuary-reports-85-percent-success-rate.

Tucker, Jonathon. "The Most Important Relationship You'll Ever Have." *The Purpose Cycle (*blog). February 14, 2021. https://www.thepurposecycle.com/post/the-most-important-relationship-you-ll-ever-have.

Wachowski, Lana, and Lilly Wachowski, dir. *The Matrix.* 1999; United States: Warner Bros.

CHAPTER 3

Middleton, Ant. *The Fear Bubble: Harness Fear and Live without Limits.* London: HarperCollins Publishers, 2020.

Oxford English Dictionary. 2nd ed. s.v. "neuroplasticity" Accessed September 30, 2020. https://www.oxfordreference.com/view/10.1093/oi/authority.20110803100230276.

Sethi, Ramit. *I Will Teach You to Be Rich.* New York: Workman Publishing Company, 2021.

CHAPTER 5

Bagley, Benjamin. "Loving Someone in Particular." *Ethics* 125, no. 2 (January 2015): 477–507.

Guthrie, K. "Self-Esteem: How to Get It and Keep It." *Counseling Center—University of Illinois Springfield.* Accessed July 7, 2021. https://www.uis.edu/counselingcenter/counselorscorner/selfesteem/.

Hoy, Sir Chris. "Chris Hoy on the Mindset to Become Olympic Champ, Never Giving up & the Father Christmas Syndrome!" Nov 16, 2020. In *High Performance.* Produced by J. Humphrey, and D. Hughes. Podcast. https://www.thehighperformancepodcast.com/episodes/sir-chris-hoy.

Hudler, Rex. *Splinters: A Memoir.* Tustin, CA: Rex Hudler, 2008.

Kirkpatrick, David. *The Facebook Effect: The Inside Story of the Company That Is Connecting the World.* New York: Simon & Schuster, 2011.

Larsen, Knud S., Harry J. Martin, Richard H. Ettinger, and Joan Nelson. "Approval Seeking, Social Cost, and Aggression: A Scale and Some Dynamics." *The Journal of Psychology* 94, no. 1 (1976): 3-11. https://doi10.1080/00223980.1976.9921389.

Nickerson, Raymond S. "Confirmation Bias: A Ubiquitous Phenomenon in Many Guises." *Review Of General Psychology,* no. 2 (1998): 175–220.

Wachowski, Lana, and Lilly Wachowski, dir. *The Matrix.* 1999; United States: Warner Bros.

Widener, Chris. *Jim Rohn's 8 Best Success Lessons*. Seattle: Made For Success Incorporated, 2014.

CHAPTER 6

Beaton, Connor. "WTF Is Holding Space. (A Man's Guide)." *Connorbeaton.Com* (blog). Accessed August 30, 2021. https://connorbeaton.com/wtf-holding-space-mans-guide/.

CHAPTER 7

Dunning, David, Kerri Johnson, Joyce Ehrlinger, and Justin Kruger. "Why People Fail to Recognize Their Own Incompetence." *Current Directions In Psychological Science* 12, no.3 (2003): 83-87.

McConaughey, Matthew. *Greenlights: Raucous Stories and Outlaw Wisdom from the Academy Award-winning Actor*. London: Headline Publishing Group, 2020.

Muccino, Gabriele, dir. *The Pursuit of Happyness*. 2006; United States: Columbia Pictures.

Proctor, Bob. *You Were Born Rich: Now You Can Discover and Develop Those Riches*. Scottsdale, AZ: Proctor Gallagher Institute, 2010.

Sinek, Simon. *Leaders Eat Last: Why Some Teams Pull Together and Others Don't*. New York: Portfolio/Penguin, 2014.

Van Sant, Gus, dir. *Good Will Hunting*. 1997; United States: Miramax. DVD.

Ziskin, Laura, et al. dir. *Spider-Man.* 2002; Culver City, California: Columbia TriStar Home Entertainment.

CHAPTER 8

Clear, James. *Atomic Habits: Tiny Changes, Remarkable Results: an Easy & Proven Way to Build Good Habits & Break Bad Ones.* New York: Penguin Random House, 2018.

Goggins, David. *Can't Hurt Me: Master Your Mind and Defy the Odds.* Muskego, Wisconsin: Lioncrest Publishing, 2018.

Lasseter, John, dir. *Toy Story.* 1995; United States: Buena Vista Pictures.

"Punishment, Comparative Cognition Laboratory, Psychological and Brain Sciences." *Psychology.Uiowa.Edu.* Accessed September 19, 2021. https://psychology.uiowa.edu/comparative-cognition-laboratory/glossary/punishment.

Tygielski, Shelly. *Sit Down to Rise Up: How Radical Self-Care Can Change the World.* Novato, California: New World Library, 2021.

CHAPTER 9

Clear, James. *Atomic Habits: Tiny Changes, Remarkable Results: an Easy & Proven Way to Build Good Habits & Break Bad Ones.* New York: Penguin Random House, 2018.

Dickinson, Kevin. "Do Participation Trophies Hinder Child Development?" *Bigthink.Com.* Accessed October 7, 2021. https://

bigthink.com/neuropsych/participation-trophy-and-child-development/#rebelltitem1.

Durant, Will. *The Story of Philosophy: The Lives and Opinions of the Great Philosophers of the Western World.* New York: Simon and Schuster, 1961.

CHAPTER 10

Abrams, Abigail. "Yes, Impostor Syndrome Is Real. Here's How to Deal With It." Accessed September 10, 2021. *Time.* https://time.com/5312483/how-to-deal-with-impostor-syndrome/.

Beet, Joshua. "Level up and Change Your Life—Josh Beet." February 22, 2021. In *The Purpose Cycle Podcast.* Produced by Jonathon Tucker. Podcast, MP3 audio. https://podcasts.apple.com/gb/podcast/level-up-and-transform-your-life-josh-beet-part-1/id1550551894?i=1000510116454.

Deleeuw, Candice. *Hope (Amidst the Stories I Told Myself).* Charlotte, NC: Self-Published—Hope in Healing Hearts, 2020.

MMAWeekly.com. "Conor McGregor: 'Mystic Mac Strikes Again.'" December 20, 2015. Video, 2:11. https://www.youtube.com/watch?v=8G1B7UzLtlk.

Middleton, Ant. *The Fear Bubble: Harness Fear and Live without Limits.* London: HarperCollins Publishers, 2020.

Sethi, Ramit. *I Will Teach You to Be Rich.* New York: Workman Publishing Company, 2021.

CHAPTER 11

Billian, Rumeet, and Todd Humber. "The Tallest Poppy: High-Performing Women Pay a Steep Price for Success." *Women Of Influence.* Accessed September 21, 2021. https://www.womenofinfluence.ca/2018/09/24/the-tallest-poppy-high-performing-women-pay-a-steep-price-for-success/.

Docherty, Shaun "Life After War—Shaun Docherty." March 1, 2021. In *The Purpose Cycle Podcast.* Produced by Jonathon Tucker. Podcast, MP3 audio. https://open.spotify.com/episode/3UxnaNTFfhbBzg6vLHAhbk?si=cU_HR8sOQJa6Ox-05PMbLwQ&dl_branch=1.

Dougherty, Morgan. "How Our Reliance of Technology Leads to a Lack of Rhetoric and Ability to Communicate." *Rhetoric & Civic Life* (blog). September 5, 2013. https://sites.psu.edu/dougherty1314rcl/2013/09/05/how-our-reliance-of-technology-leads-to-a-lack-of-rhetoric/.

Julson, Erica. "10 Best Ways to Increase Dopamine Levels Naturally." *Healthline.* Accessed May 17, 2021. https://www.healthline.com/nutrition/how-to-increase-dopamine#TOC_TITLE_HDR_8.

Mathers, Connie. "Trust the Process: 8 Ways to Use This Mantra in Your Life." *Develop Good Habits.* Accessed July 19, 2021. https://www.developgoodhabits.com/trust-the-process/.

Muccino, Gabriele, dir. *The Pursuit of Happyness.* 2006; United States: Columbia Pictures.

"Naval Ravikant on Happiness, Reducing Anxiety, Crypto Stablecoins, and Crypto Strategy." October 2020. In *The Tim Ferriss*

Show #473. Podcast, MP3 audio. https://tim.blog/2020/10/14/naval/.

Proctor, Bob. *You Were Born Rich: Now You Can Discover and Develop Those Riches.* Scottsdale, AZ: Proctor Gallagher Institute, 2010.

Sinek, Simon. *The Infinite Game.* London, England: Portfolio Penguin, 2020.

"Take Control of Your Health with No-Nonsense News on Lifestyle, Gut Microbes and Genetics." *Atlas Biomed* (blog). Accessed July 21, 2021. https://atlasbiomed.com/blog/serotonin-and-other-happy-molecules-made-by-gut-bacteria/.

CHAPTER 13

Proctor, Bob. *You Were Born Rich: Now You Can Discover and Develop Those Riches.* Scottsdale. AZ: Proctor Gallagher Institute, 2010.

Rigsby, Rick. *Lessons from a Third Grade Dropout: How the Timeless Wisdom of One Man Can Impact an Entire Generation.* London: Thomas Nelson, 2019.

Zeal, Kylie. *Seven Freedom Elements: The Essential Foundations for Confidence, Clarity and a Life You Love.* New York: Morgan James Publishing, 2017.

CHAPTER 14

García, Héctor, and Francesc Miralles. *Ikigai: The Japanese Secret to a Long and Happy Life.* London: Random House, 2017.

Goleman, Daniel. *Emotional Intelligence: Why It Can Matter More Than IQ.* London: Random House Publishing Group, 2012.

Lautin, Andrew L. *The Limbic Brain.* New York: Springer US, 2013.

Mitsuhashi, Y Yukari. "Ikigai: A Japanese Concept to Improve Work and Life." *BBC Worklife,* August 8, 2017. https://www.bbc.com/worklife/article/20170807-ikigai-a-japanese-concept-to-improve-work-and-life.

Tucker, Jonathon. "Developing Emotional Intelligence. "*The Purpose Cycle* (blog). August 16, 2021. https://www.thepurposecycle.com/post/developing-emotional-intelligence.